Massachusetts

OUR HOME

Gibbs Smith, Publisher

ABOUT THE AUTHORS

Mary Stockwell, Ph.D. is the Chairperson of the Department of History at Lourdes College. She teaches courses in American and World History. She has developed new courses in Native American History, the Civil War and Reconstruction, and the United States in the Twentieth Century. She especially enjoys teaching Colonial and Revolutionary America, a class where Massachusetts plays an important part. Many of her students become teachers in grade school and high school. She also serves on the Education Advisory Board for her college. Dr. Stockwell has written about the history and economics of the United States and the rest of the world for many encyclopedias. She is currently working on a biography of President Woodrow Wilson that will be part of a series of books called *First Men, America's Presidents.*

Courtney Johnson Thomas is an author and editor with a Master's degree in English. She works with historians, reading specialists, authors, editors, and artists to publish quality history textbooks for elementary and secondary students. For the past seven years she has helped produce state-history textbooks for schools across the country. She has also worked on the school tour committee at the Emily Dickinson Museum in Amherst.

CONTRIBUTORS AND REVIEWERS

Annawon Weeden is a Native American Program Specialist for the Children's Museum of Boston, and a member of the Mashpee Wampanoag Tribe on Cape Cod. Mr. Weeden's current duties include conducting programs for visiting schools and developing curriculum for education around Wampanoag culture. His prior experience includes interpreting history at Plimoth Plantation as well as creating exhibits for various museums such as the Mashantucket Pequot Museum and Research Center and schools in the New England area.

Judy Battat is the Native Projects Manager at the Children's Museum of Boston. She collaborates with educators and members of the Native American community to create professional development opportunities for teachers. She shared an early copy of this manuscript with teacher participants in a Children's Museum professional development summer institute, "Many Thanksgivings, An Immersion Into Wampanoag Seasonal Celebrations." Ms. Battat has prior experience in museums including Old Sturbridge Village and the People and Places Program of the Boston Freedom Trail and Black Heritage Trail Museums. She also has a Master's degree in Multicultural Education. She has worked with students with special needs and is certified in elementary and special education.

Robert Lacey is a doctoral student in political science at the University of Massachusetts at Amherst. He teaches courses in American government and political thought and works as a researcher for the university's Donahue Institute.

Published by
Gibbs Smith, Publisher
P.O. Box 667
Layton, UT 84041
800-748-5439
www.gibbs-smith.com/textbooks

Managing Editor: Courtney Johnson Thomas
Associate Editors: Susan Myers, Carrie Gibson
Editorial Assistants: Jennifer Petersen, Valerie Hatch
Cover and Book Design: Alan Connell
Maps and Graphs: Alan Connell

Cover photo: The lantern, made of tinned iron and glass, has been identified as one of the two that hung in the belfry of Christ Church (the Old North Church) on the night of April 18, 1775. The lanterns were a signal to the local militia that the British were leaving Boston by water. That night Paul Revere made his famous ride to warn the people that the British were coming. The lantern was probably made in England, circa 1765-1775. Courtesy of The Concord Museum; Concord, Massachusetts; www.concordmuseum.org.

Printed and bound in China.

ISBN 10 : 1-58685-059-8

ISBN 13 : 978-1-58685-059-3

10 09 08 10 9 8

This book is dedicated to the memory of Elizabeth Stockwell, and to the students and teachers of Massachusetts. You are the future not only of our state but of our nation and the world. Try to think as far as your heart and imagination will take you. Use the lessons of our past to build a better future for everyone.

Contents

Maps

Activities & Skills

Massachusetts Portraits

State Symbols

It is fun to learn about Massachusetts through our state symbols. Each symbol shows something special about our state. School children from Massachusetts helped choose some of our state symbols. Can you guess which ones they voted for?

State Dog: Boston Terrier

Our state dog is very smart. It loves to play and is a great companion. It is part bulldog and part English terrier. It is brown and white or black and white with a short shiny coat. Do you see its pointed ears?

State Tree: American Elm

Under the branches of this stately tree, George Washington first led the American army. Elm trees can grow to be 120 feet tall. Their leaves are dark green. They turn yellow in the fall. Elm trees grow very fast and can live in almost any climate.

State Cat: Tabby Cat

School children chose the tabby cat as our state cat. The word "tabby" describes the pattern of the cat's fur. Different types of cats can have tabby markings. The most common tabby markings look like tiger stripes. Tabby cats are orange, brown, silver, gray, or black.

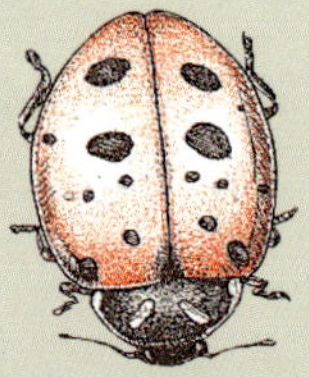

State Insect: Ladybug

Did you know that four ladybugs named after the Beatles (John, Paul, George, and Ringo) once rode on the space shuttle? They were part of an experiment. Back on Earth, ladybugs are good for your garden because they eat other bugs. Making ladybugs our state insect was the idea of second graders in Franklin, Massachusetts.

State Fish: Cod

The cod is our state fish. Long ago, explorers sailed along the coast. One explorer found so many cod, his men could pull them from the ocean in baskets. Soon, fishermen were sailing to the waters around Massachusetts. A sailor named Cape Cod after all the fish he found there.

State Bird: Black-Capped Chickadee
State Flower: Mayflower

Our state bird and flower are alike in many ways. Both are small and delicate. The chickadee is only four to five inches tall. It likes to stay close to the ground. It makes its nest in tree stumps or fence posts.

The mayflower lives close to the ground too. It grows in the woods under or near evergreen trees. The petals of a mayflower are small and soft. Sometimes the flower is called ground laurel.

Our flower and bird are also different from one another. The mayflower is bright pink or white and is not seen very often. The chickadee is gray, black, and white. It is seen all over North America.

State Muffin: Corn Muffin

Not many states have a state muffin, but we do! The corn muffin has been an important food in New England for hundreds of years. This state symbol was also chosen by school children.

State Beverage: Cranberry Juice

Did you know Massachusetts grows one of the largest cranberry crops in the world? That is why cranberry juice is our state beverage. Cranberries have been used for hundreds of years. Native Americans ate them, used them as medicine, and made them into dye for blankets and rugs. There is even a museum in Plymouth called Cranberry World.

State Marine Mammal: Right Whale

This big, slow-moving mammal spends more time near the shore than most other whales. That is why early whalers hunted and killed almost all of them. Today, their numbers are slowly growing again. A right whale can live for over 60 years. Its large head is covered with bumps, and it is black or dark gray in color. It swims with its mouth open so it can eat all the time.

Our State Flag and Seal

Our state flag stands for all the people of Massachusetts. It shows that no matter how different we are from each other, we are united in our love of our state and our freedom.

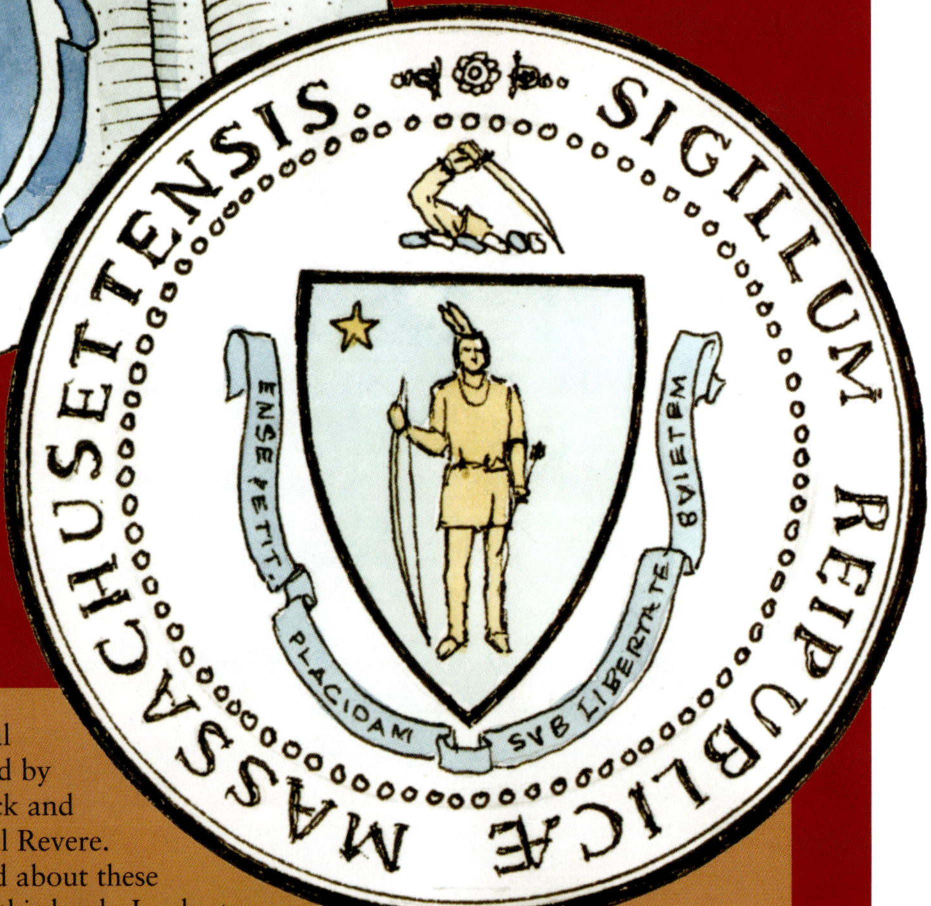

Our state seal was approved by John Hancock and made by Paul Revere. You will read about these men later in this book. Look at the words around the outside of the seal. They are Latin for "Seal of the Republic of Massachusetts." Do you see a strong arm holding a sword? It goes with the words on the banner. These words mean, "By the sword we seek peace, but peace only under liberty." Do you see a Native American man? He is holding his bow pointed down as a sign of peace. Now find the star. It shows that Massachusetts was one of the first 13 colonies.

Our State Song

"All Hail to Massachusetts"
by Arthur J. Marsh
Official Song of the Commonwealth

All hail to Massachusetts, the land of the free and the brave!
For Bunker Hill and Charlestown, and flag we love to wave;
For Lexington and Concord, and the shot heard 'round the world;
All hail to Massachusetts, we'll keep her flag unfurled.
She stands upright for freedom's light that shines from sea to sea;
All hail to Massachusetts! Our country 'tis of thee!

All hail to grand old Bay State, the home of the bean and the cod,
Where pilgrims found a landing and gave their thanks to God.
A land of opportunity in the good old U.S.A.
Where men live long and prosper, and people come to stay.
Don't sell her short but learn to court her industry and stride;
All hail to grand old Bay State! The land of pilgrim's pride!

All hail to Massachusetts, renowned in the Hall of Fame!
How proudly wave her banners emblazoned with her name!
In unity and brotherhood, sons and daughters go hand in hand;
All hail to Massachusetts, there is no finer land!
It's M-A-S-S-A-C-H-U-S-E-T-T-S.
All hail to Massachusetts! All hail! All hail! All hail!

History Close to Home

History is what happened in the past. It is about the people of the past. It is about the big things they did, like going to war or inventing something. It is also about the little things they did every day.

This woman is making a basket by hand, just like the Puritans in Salem did long ago.

- *Why do you think she is making her own baskets? How do people today get baskets and other things they need?*
- *Find the little girl in the picture. What is she wearing? How are her clothes different from the clothes we wear today?*
- *Do you see the fence in the background? What do you think it was made of? What do you think the house was made of? How are our fences and homes different today?*

Chapter 1

If you visit Pioneer Village in Salem, you can see how people lived about 400 years ago.

Photo ©Kindra Clineff

Lesson 1

Local History

WORDS TO UNDERSTAND
character
community
history
local
museum

What Is History?

Have you ever been to a ***museum?*** Have your grandparents told you stories about when they were kids? Have you read a book about a hero from long ago? All of these things have to do with the past. The past is everything that has happened up until this very moment.

History is the story of the past. It is the story of what people thought, how they lived, and what choices they made.

What Is Local History?

In this book we will study local history. ***Local*** means close to home. We will study the history of Massachusetts. We will learn about its place in New England.

We will also learn about your town or city and your ***community.*** A community is a group of people living and working together. You will learn how history was made in your community.

Activity

Know Your Town

It is fun to learn about the place where you live. What do you already know about your town's history? As a class, make a list on the chalkboard. See how many things you can write down. They can be things that happened last month, five years ago, or 200 years ago.

Don't worry if your list is not very long. If you do this again when you finish this book, your list will be much longer!

My Town

1.

2.

3.

YOUR TOWN

As you read this book, you will have a chance to explore history near you. From time to time you will see this sign. It will remind you to look for history in your own town or city.

This family is learning about the past by visiting a monument in Boston.

Drawing by Shauna Kawasaki

Has anyone ever said you are a good worker? Do you tell the truth? Has someone said you are kind? All of this has to do with ***character.*** *People have always faced challenges. Their character helped them through hard times. In this picture, students are putting on a play about history. See if you can find people showing good character by working together.*

What Makes History Happen?

History did not have to turn out the way it did. Much of the past is the way it is because of choices people made. They chose how to solve problems and how to treat one another.

History is not always peaceful. Sometimes people worked well together. Sometimes they fought or did bad things to each other. We can look back and see what mistakes people made. We can learn from those mistakes. We can also learn from the good choices people made.

We can see how our lives are different from the lives of people who lived long ago. We can also learn how they are the same. By studying history, we begin to understand who we are.

Lesson 1

Memory Master

1. What is local history?
2. Why do we study local history?

Lesson 2

How We Study History

How do we study history? There are many ways we can learn about the past. Let's read about some of them.

Study Artifacts

One way we can learn about the past is by looking at things people used every day. An ***artifact*** is something made or used by people of the past.

For example, a Native American basket is an artifact. By looking at the basket, we might learn what grasses and other plants the people had. We might be able to tell if they carried water or gathered berries in the basket. This would tell us something about their lives.

Artifacts can tell us how people lived. They can show us how life has changed. Museums are places where artifacts are kept. People can visit museums to learn more about the past.

Have you ever seen an artifact in a museum?

Activity

Artifacts Tell a Story

When you need butter for your toast or pancakes, where do you get it? Long ago, people had to make their own butter. They used a butter churn.

To make butter, they put cream in the bottom part. They used the pole to stir the cream. As they stirred, the cream got thicker. It took a lot of stirring to turn the cream into butter!

Look closely at the butter churn and answer the questions.

1. What was the churn made from?
2. Describe how it looks. What color is it? Is it smooth or rough? Does it have any parts that move?
3. Who might have used it?
4. Where might it have been used?
5. What does it tell us about the life and times of the people who used it?
6. Is there anything we use today that is like this?

How Do We Know?

PEOPLE TO KNOW

Deborah Samson

PLACES TO LOCATE

Boston
Deerfield
Middleborough
Plymouth
Plympton

WORDS TO UNDERSTAND

artifact
biography
century
courage
decade
heroine
historic site
pension
pioneer
time period

Read a Biography

History is made by people. We can learn about people by reading about their lives. A ***biography*** is a story of a person's life. A biography is not a made-up story. It is based on facts.

Read this short biography of Deborah Samson. Then answer the questions at the right.

Read more about Deborah Samson! See if you can find biographies of her in the library or on the Internet.

Massachusetts also has a state hero. Find out who he was and read about his life.

Massachusetts
PORTRAIT

Deborah Samson

State Heroine of Massachusetts

1760–1827

Deborah Samson is our state ***heroine.*** A heroine is a woman who is admired for what she did. Here is her story.

On the Farm

Deborah Samson was from Plympton. Her family was poor. When she was very young, her father left the family. Her mother had to send her to live with another family.

Deborah lived with a farmer and worked on his farm. He had ten sons, so she was the only girl. She grew tall and strong from all the hard work. She did not get to go to school, but each night the boys taught her what they had learned that day.

Teaching Others

Deborah became a teacher. She taught in a small schoolhouse in Middleborough. To make extra money, she spun yarn and wove cloth in other people's homes and at a tavern.

During this time, Americans were fighting a war with England. The last big battle was over, but there was still some fighting. Everyone was talking about it. Deborah heard stories of brave soldiers and their adventures.

1. What decisions did Deborah Samson make that were important in her life?
2. Think of three words that describe her.
3. Pretend you are Deborah Samson. You are camped near a battlefield. Write a letter to a friend at home telling what you see, hear, and feel.

A Soldier's Secret

Deborah knew that women were not allowed to be soldiers. She dressed up as a man and signed up to fight. She wrote her name as Robert Shirtliff.

Deborah (Robert) was a tough, strong soldier. Once a sword cut her on the side of the head. She was also shot in the leg. After her head was bandaged, she limped out of the hospital. She did not want the doctor to find out her secret. She tried to take the musket ball out of her leg using her own knife.

Later, Deborah got sick and had to see another doctor. This doctor found out that "Robert" was really a woman. He didn't tell anyone. Instead, he took her to his home so he and his wife could help her get better.

Sharing Her Story

After the war, Deborah Samson got married and had three children. They were very poor. Her friend Paul Revere wanted to help her, since she had helped the country. He asked the government to give her some money to live on, called a ***pension.*** He wrote, "Her husband is a good sort of man, though of small force in business. They have a few acres of poor land, . . . but they are really poor."

Deborah found another way to make money. She traveled to many cities to speak about her life.

A State Heroine

Many years after she died, Deborah Samson became the state heroine of Massachusetts. We remember her today for her ***courage*** in the past.

At Historic Deerfield you can learn all about how pioneer families lived. You can play pioneer games and practice spinning wool on a real spinning wheel.

An old home can be a historic site. It can tell us a lot about how life used to be. Paul Revere's home is a historic site in Boston. He did something important that helped to make history. Do you know what it was? You will learn about him in a later chapter.

Visit a Historic Site

Our state has many *historic sites.* These are places where history happened. Some historic sites might be in your town.

Many towns also have a historical society. This is a special place where artifacts and records are kept.

Ask Questions

We can ask lots of questions when we study history. We can ask:

- What happened?
- When did it happen?
- Who took part in it?
- Why did it happen?
- How did it change things?

Can you think of any other questions you could ask to learn about our past?

Plimoth Plantation is where the Pilgrims first settled. Much later, people made it look just like it did when the Pilgrims lived there.

Century:	18th	19th	20th	21st
	▼	▼	▼	▼
Years:	1700s	1800s	1900s	2000

Hint: To know the century, go up one number.
For example, 1600s = 17th century.

Understand Time Periods

What is today's date? What was yesterday's date? What was the date when you were born? When we talk about history, we often use dates. Dates tell us when things happened.

In this book you will learn some important dates in our state's history. You will learn how to use dates when you speak and write about history. Here are some words we use to talk about time:

A ***time period*** is a chunk of time. Time periods help us talk about the past.

A ***decade*** is 10 years. For example, the 90s were a decade. Talk with your class about something that happened in the 1990s.

A ***century*** is 100 years. This book was made in the year 2004. One hundred years ago it was 1904. Look in the library or on the Internet to find something that happened about that time.

What century are you living in now?

When people talk about the 20th century, they are talking about the 1900s. When we talk about the 19th century, we are talking about the 1800s, and so forth. Look at the chart above to see how this works. What century are we learning about if we are studying about the 1600s?

Lesson 2

Memory Master

1. List three ways you can learn about the past.
2. What is a biography?
3. What is a decade?

Chapter 1 Review

What's the Point?

History is the story of the people of the past. By studying local history, we can see how people's choices changed our state, town, or city. We can learn about ourselves. We can try to build a better future.

Activity

Make History!

Each one of us is a part of history. We are all important in the history of our family, community, town, and state. When you put your trash in the garbage can or recycle bin, you help protect our land. When you collect food for people who are hungry, you help solve a problem in your community. When you welcome someone from a different place, you help to make the American dream come true.

Have someone in your class write this sentence on the chalkboard:

What you do today is the history of tomorrow.

As a class, talk about what this means. What can you do today that will help make history?

Activity

Hunt for Artifacts

Find a museum or historic site near you. Go for a visit. See if you can find an artifact. Look closely at it and answer these questions.

1. What is it?
2. What was it used for?
3. Who would have used it?
4. During what time did the people live? In what century did they live?

Activity

Brainstorm: More Ways to Study History

In this chapter we learned some ways we can study history. Can you think of any other ways? Brainstorm with your class. Have someone write all the ideas on the chalkboard.

What is the land like in Massachusetts? Who are the people who live here? How do they use the land to make a living?

Farming is one way people in Northfield make a living. They grow apples and other crops to sell. Have you ever picked an apple right off a tree? Do you like to drink cider in the fall?

Chapter

2

The Land We Call Home

"Nature always wears the colors of the spirit."

—Ralph Waldo Emerson

Photo ©Kindra Clineff

Lesson 1

New England

PLACES TO LOCATE

New England
Connecticut
Maine
Massachusetts
New Hampshire
Rhode Island
Vermont
Atlantic Ocean

WORDS TO UNDERSTAND

cardinal directions
goods
harbor
map legend
mill
natural resource
scale of miles
services
suburb
symbol

History and the Land

When we study local history, where should we start? We can start by learning about the land. The land has a lot to do with how people have lived here. It has to do with the foods people grew, the clothes they wore, and the kinds of homes they built.

A Place Called New England

Captain John Smith was an explorer long ago. He was from England. As a young man he had seen many places. He helped to settle Virginia. Later, he visited a place he named Massachusetts.

To John Smith, no land seemed as beautiful as Massachusetts. It was part of a bigger area he named New England.

As Smith and his crew sailed along the coast, they found many good ***harbors.*** A harbor is a protected place near the shore where the water is deep enough for large ships. Many fish swam around Smith's ship. He saw woods to the west. Hawks swooped above him in the bright blue sky. There were Native American villages along the shore.

John Smith named Massachusetts. He got the name from a group of Native Americans. They were called the Massachusett. They lived at a place called the Great Blue Hill. The word Massachusett *means "people who live near the big hill."*

New England sits next to the Atlantic Ocean. Today, you can see lighthouses along the coast. Lighthouses help ship captains see where the land is.

Water is a natural resource in New England. At a **mill,** people used the power of a rushing river to move heavy stones that ground grain into flour. Water power also moved the saws that cut logs into boards. Before long, people were using water to run machines. The machines made cloth. Mills became large factories.

▲ Photo ©Tom Till

The ocean is a natural resource. It gives us fish and shellfish to eat.

New England's Resources

When we say "New England" today, we are talking about six states: Maine, New Hampshire, Vermont, Massachusetts, Connecticut, and Rhode Island. You can find them on the map on page 21.

The land in New England has a lot to offer. There are many ***natural resources*** here. These are things found in nature that people use. New England has:

- **Forests** Many animals live in the forests. People also use the forests. They cut down trees and use the wood to make homes, furniture, toys, and paper. In Maine, Christmas trees are grown and shipped to people in other places. People like to hike or camp in the forests. Have you ever been for a walk in the woods?

- **Water** New England is next to the Atlantic Ocean. It also has many rivers. The first people to live here used the ocean and rivers to find fish and shellfish. Today, there are fisheries where fish is canned or frozen, then sold to stores. People come from all over the world to eat New England lobsters, clams, cod, flounder, haddock, and sea scallops. People have always used the water for travel and for fun.

- **Soil** Some places in New England have good soil for farming. Farmers grow apples, potatoes, corn, tobacco, and other crops. Massachusetts is known for its cranberries. Maine is known for its blueberries. Much of the land is good for dairy farming. Dairy farmers sell milk, cheese, butter, eggs—and sometimes home-made ice cream.

- **Minerals** New England has sand, gravel, stone, marble, clay, quartz, and other minerals that people use. Two minerals found in Connecticut are copper and limestone. Copper is used to make wire and pennies. It gives color to green paint. It is also polished and sold as jewelry. Limestone is used to make cement and steel. Rhode Island has granite and crushed stone. They are used for building. Massachusetts has sand, gravel, crushed stone, and other minerals.

The People of New England

Today, the people in New England have lots of choices about where to live. Many people live in big cities. Others live in the *suburbs.* Suburbs are places outside the city with houses, yards, and shopping malls. Some people live in small towns. Some live on farms. Some live in fishing villages.

People have to earn a living. They need to earn money to buy the things they need. To earn a living, many people buy and sell goods. *Goods* are things that people make to sell. In New England, people make maple syrup. They make cranberry juice from cranberries. They make books and build submarines. Can you think of other goods made in New England?

Services are things that people do for other people. They earn money by selling their services. For example, fixing a computer is a service. Coaching a baseball team is a service. People need care from doctors and nurses. They need education from teachers. In New England, many people work in education. There are very fine colleges here. Some people work at museums or places that serve food. These are all services.

We will learn more about goods and services in Chapter 7.

People who live in New England work in all kinds of jobs. What goods and services do you see in these pictures?

Reading a Map

There are many kinds of maps. Can you think of some? Maybe you thought of a treasure map! Maybe you thought of the road maps your parents use on trips.

Maps help us know where we are. They help us get where we want to go.

Look at this map of New England. The red boxes point to tools that help us read a map.

Activity

New England on the Map

Use the map to answer the questions:

1. What is the title of the map?
2. What do the symbols on the map stand for?
3. Use the legend to find the New England states. How many are there? What are their names?
4. Find the compass. Name a state that is south of Massachusetts.
5. Find the scale of miles. How many miles are equal to one inch?
6. How many miles are between Boston and Hartford?
7. How many miles are between Providence and Augusta?
8. Which is the longer distance?

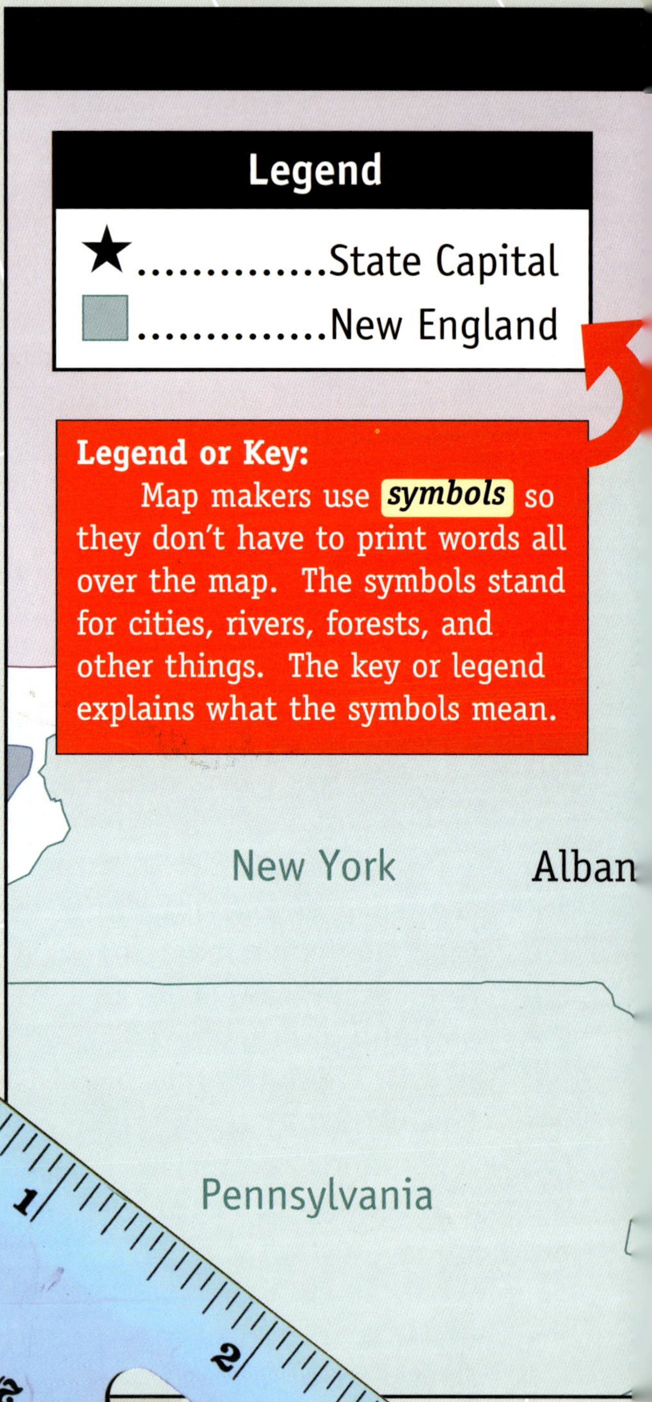

Lesson 1 Memory Master

1. Tell one thing you learned about the land in New England.
2. Tell one thing you learned about the people of New England.
3. What ocean is next to New England?
4. List the cardinal directions.

Title:

The first thing to look for is the title. It is usually at the top. It tells you what kind of information the map shows.

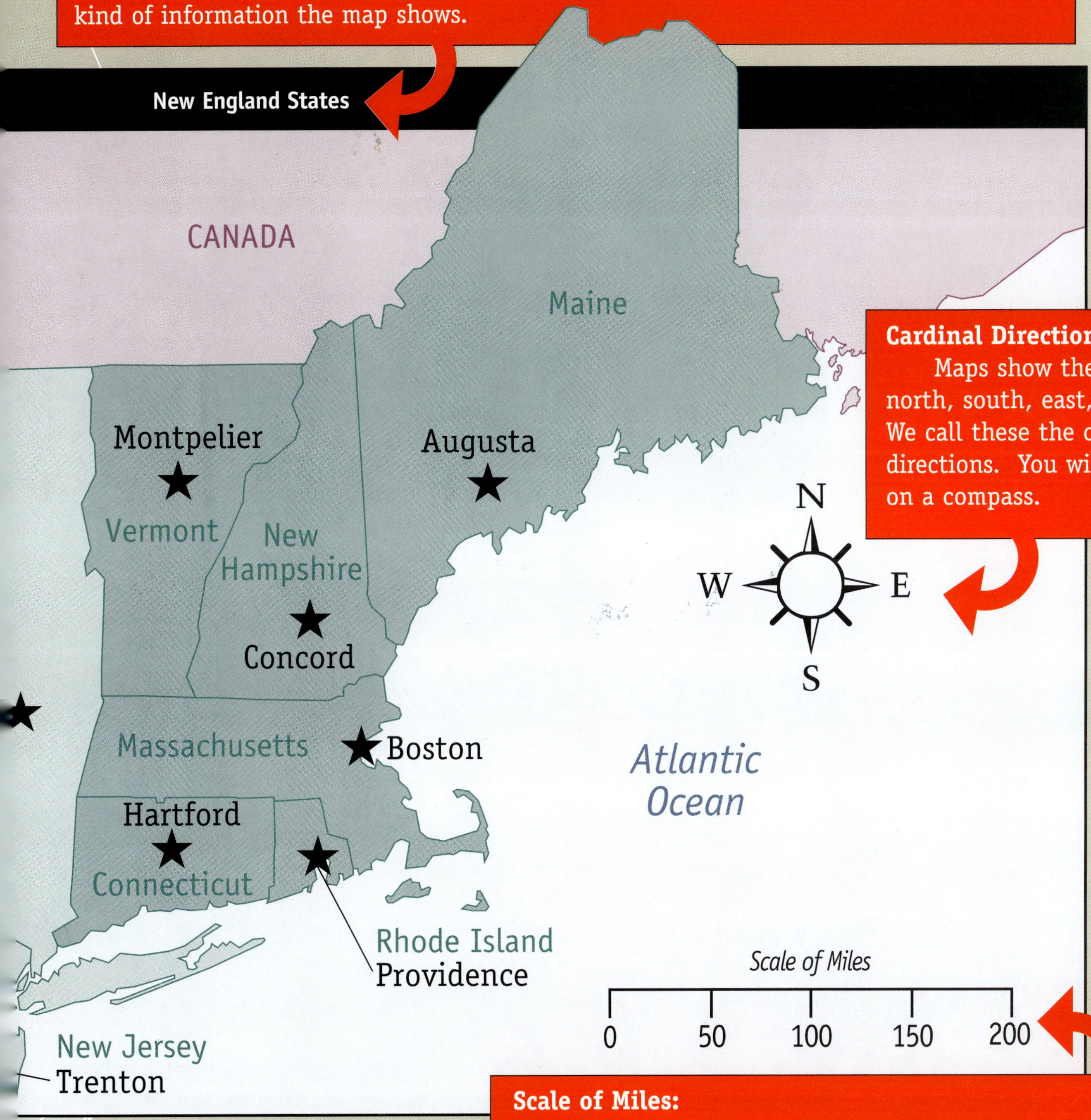

Cardinal Directions:

Maps show the directions north, south, east, and west. We call these the cardinal directions. You will find them on a compass.

Scale of Miles:

To show us how far apart things are, map makers use a scale of miles. This helps us measure the distance between places.

One inch on a map might stand for 100 miles on real land. Or one inch might mean 1,000 miles or even more.

Lesson 2

Massachusetts

PLACES TO LOCATE

Massachusetts
Cape Ann
Cape Cod
North Shore
South Shore
Pioneer Valley
Berkshire Hills
Boston
New Bedford
Springfield
Worcester
Charles River
Connecticut River
Merrimack River

WORDS TO UNDERSTAND

ancestor
cape
ceramic
endangered species
geography
graze
island
monadnock
reservoir
transportation
valley

Photo of Irish Girls ©Kindra Clineff ◄

A Place Called Massachusetts

In many ways, Massachusetts looks like it did when John Smith first saw it. It sits beside the Atlantic Ocean. It has many miles of coastline. The sandy shores of Cape Cod still stretch out to the sea. Forests head west as far as the eye can see.

Smith saw land that had been cleared so crops could grow. He knew that hunters and fishermen were changing the land and water. But Massachusetts has changed even more than Smith could have thought. It is a place with big cities and small towns. Workers make goods for the whole world to buy. Farmers send fruit, milk, cheese, and tobacco to people everywhere.

The people of our state come from many different backgrounds. Their ***ancestors*** came from Ireland, Africa, Spain, Portugal, Italy, Asia, and many other nations. You could probably find people from almost every place in the world living in Massachusetts!

There are newspapers in many languages. Have you ever seen a newspaper in Cambodian or Chinese? How about Spanish, Japanese, Portuguese, Russian, or Swedish?

People Use the Rivers

Water is very important to us. All living things need water.

Massachusetts has many rivers. A long time ago, rivers made *transportation* easier. It was easier to float down a river than to clear trees to make a road. In the past, rushing water was used to power machines. The machines made goods that were sold to other places.

Today, many people use water for fun. They can go swimming, boating, rafting, or fishing. How do you have fun in the water?

"To put your hands in a river is to feel the cords that bind the earth together."
—Barry Lopez

What do you think?

Many of our cities were built along rivers. Can you think of some reasons why? Think about how people use the water.

Massachusetts Rivers

1. *Which river is closest to where you live?*
2. *Many of our cities are along the rivers. Boston is on the ________________ River.*
3. *Lowell is on the ________________ River.*
4. *Pittsfield is on the ________________ River.*

A Bird's-Eye View of Massachusetts

From the deck of his ship, John Smith could see the shore of Cape Cod. He could see rising hills. He could see forests to the west. If he had gone in from the shore, he might have seen that Massachusetts has many different kinds of land.

Today we can take a trip in a hot-air balloon! Let's explore our state's ***geography.*** Let's visit some of the places and meet some of the people. We will lift off at the tip of Cape Cod and move west.

Cape Cod and the islands are huge piles of sand built up from the ocean floor.

The Cape

From up here, Cape Cod looks like a great arm that curves out toward the sea. A ***cape*** is a point of land that juts out into a large body of water. Pine and oak trees grow in the sandy soil.

As the Cape curves toward the ocean, the winds pick up. They blow in hard from the sea. Few trees are strong enough to take the pounding. The pine and oak give way to tall grasses.

As the arm of Cape Cod turns in, even the tall grasses disappear. Sandy beaches stretch to the Cape's tip.

Look at the many ponds. Are those beach plums and blueberries growing along the banks? If you look closely you might see chipmunks, squirrels, and raccoons living in the tall grasses. Lobsters live in the waters near the shore. Cod and salmon swim farther out to sea. For part of the year, you can see whales in the ocean.

You can't miss all the people who come to Cape Cod for vacation. See them swimming at the beaches. See them wandering through the shops. They stop to eat some of the best seafood in the world.

Do you feel the ocean breeze? Can you taste the salty air? We're passing some ***islands.*** An island is land surrounded by water on all sides. Sandy beaches curve around Martha's Vineyard and Nantucket.

People aren't the only visitors. This area is part of a path that birds use to fly south. Geese, owls, hawks, ducks, and songbirds pass over Cape Cod. Many of the birds make the Cape their summer home.

A Day in the Life of Tim McNulty

Tim McNulty knows a lot about lobsters. He is the chef at the Lobster Pot. People from all over the world eat at this restaurant in Provincetown. They know it by the bright red lights on the sign.

Let's go back into the kitchen with Tim. When the lobsters are brought in, he sorts out which ones he wants to serve. He puts them on a scale to see how much they weigh. He measures them from claw to tail. He picks the best ones to use in many different dishes.

In the summer, the Lobster Pot serves over 1,000 meals a day. Tim makes sure the food tastes delicious and looks great too. He makes sure the cooks all do their jobs. He makes sure the servers do their jobs. Sometimes he finds time to leave the kitchen and talk to kids who are eating there. He tells them all about lobsters. When he is not at the restaurant, Tim likes to fly his airplane or go fishing.

People have been growing cranberries for hundreds of years. Native Americans, early settlers, and sailors at sea ate them to get vitamin C. Today they are the number-one food crop in our state. Most of the cranberries are grown on the South Shore.

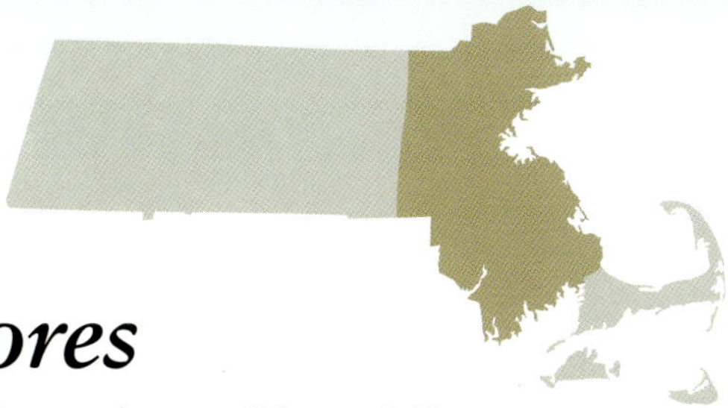

The North and South Shores

We are drifting north to another cape—Cape Ann. Listen! Do you hear the waves crashing into the rocky coast? The fishing boats look tiny from up here. For hundreds of years they have sailed from Gloucester and Salem on the North Shore. They have sailed from Plymouth and New Bedford on the South Shore.

The wind shifts, and we float south. As we pass Boston the coast becomes sandy. The first Englishmen who settled here were not happy with the land. There were big rocks everywhere. The only crop that seemed to grow was the cranberry. Many people took to the sea to make a living. Today, both cranberries and fishing are important businesses here.

Heading west, the land begins to rise. Below us are forests of maple, oak, and hickory trees.

If you flew above the North Shore, you would see harbors like this one.

The people of Gloucester are proud of their ▶ brave sailors. This statue honors them.

Heading West

The wind is steady, so we glide over Worcester. It is the second largest city in New England, after Boston. See the busy factories making everything from farm equipment to roller skates and shredded wheat. Keep a lookout for museums and colleges below.

Watch out for ***monadnocks!*** They are mountains made of rock scattered here and there.

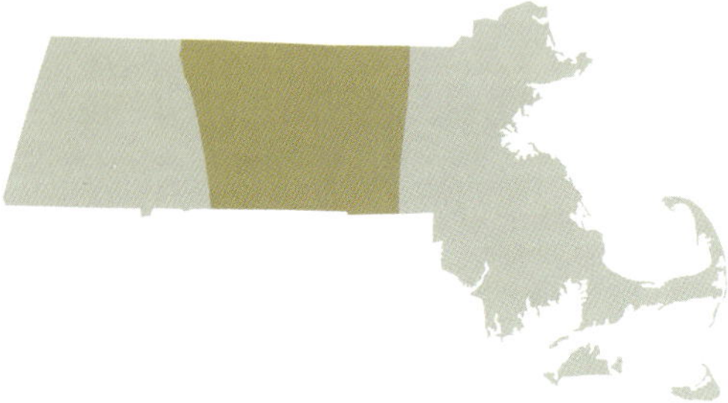

The land is rising. Watch it tumble down to the Connecticut River Valley. A ***valley*** is low land between mountains and hills. Ponds and lakes shimmer in the forests. Farms full of apples and sweet corn are nestled in the rolling hillsides. White-tailed deer roam the woods. Long ago, this land was home to bobcats, wolves, and black bears.

What is that huge lake ahead of us? It is the Quabbin Reservoir. A ***reservoir*** is a lake made by people. The Quabbin stores water for many people. A bald eagle swoops by. A coyote trots through the trees. Fish swim in the clear water.

Photo ©William H. Johnson

Photo ©Kindra Clineff

A Day in the Life of Mike Wright

Mike Wright works in a factory in Worcester.

Mike Wright gets up very early. His workday starts at 4:30 a.m., while you are still sleeping. He works in a factory called Saint-Gobain in Worcester. He makes **ceramic** bricks.

The bricks are made to last a long time. They are sold to many customers. These customers use the bricks to make ovens in other factories. The ovens get as hot as the inside of a volcano.

Many products are baked in the ovens to make them strong. For example, brick ovens are used to make tiny parts that go in computers. The sinks in your home were probably baked with Saint-Gobain products.

Mike makes sure the people he works with have everything they need to make the bricks. He sees that they make the best bricks possible. He wants his customers to be happy.

Mike goes home at 2:00 p.m. It has been a long day. He may stop to visit a friend. He also likes to watch football, especially his favorite team—the New England Patriots!

At the Quabbin Reservoir, you can see people hiking or having a picnic, but you won't see anyone swimming. It is important to keep the water clean and natural.

Would you like to walk through the trees 40 feet above the ground? You can do that at the EcoTarium in Worcester. You can learn all about trees and the environment there.

The Connecticut River Valley is also called the Pioneer Valley. Look up the word "pioneer" in the glossary. See if you can guess why the valley has this name.

The Pioneer Valley

We are heading towards a large valley. That winding river below us is the Connecticut River. Farms are spread along both sides of the river. Farmers grow apples, sweet corn, and tobacco in the rich soil. Sugar maple trees give a good supply of syrup every spring. Dairy cows ***graze*** in the meadows.

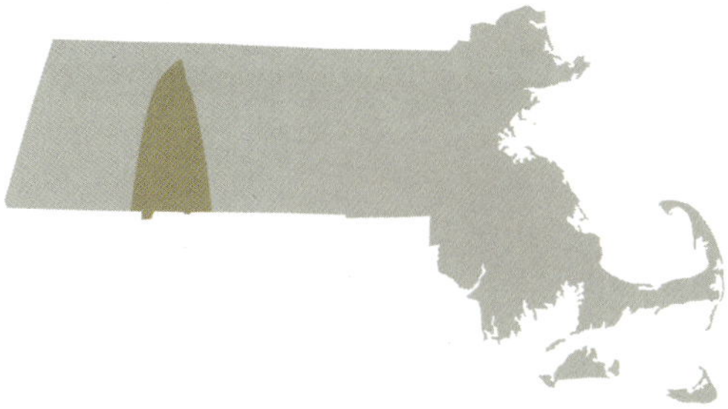

Since the early 1700s, this area has been called the Pioneer Valley. Farmers came from Boston and other towns to find richer soil. Many people trapped beavers along the Connecticut River.

Later, in the 1800s, people built mills along the river. Workers made paper from logs that were floated down from Vermont each spring.

The valley is home to some of the finest colleges in the nation, including Amherst, Smith, and Mount Holyoke Colleges.

Massachusetts
PORTRAIT

Dr. Seuss
1904–1991

Have you ever read *The Cat in the Hat*? What about *Fox in Sox* or *Green Eggs and Ham*? A man called Dr. Seuss wrote them. His real name was Theodor Seuss Geisel. He was born in Springfield. If you visit Springfield, you can see a statue of Dr. Seuss and some of the characters in his books.

Dr. Seuss wanted to make learning fun. His books teach children how to read in a fun way. What is your favorite Dr. Seuss book?

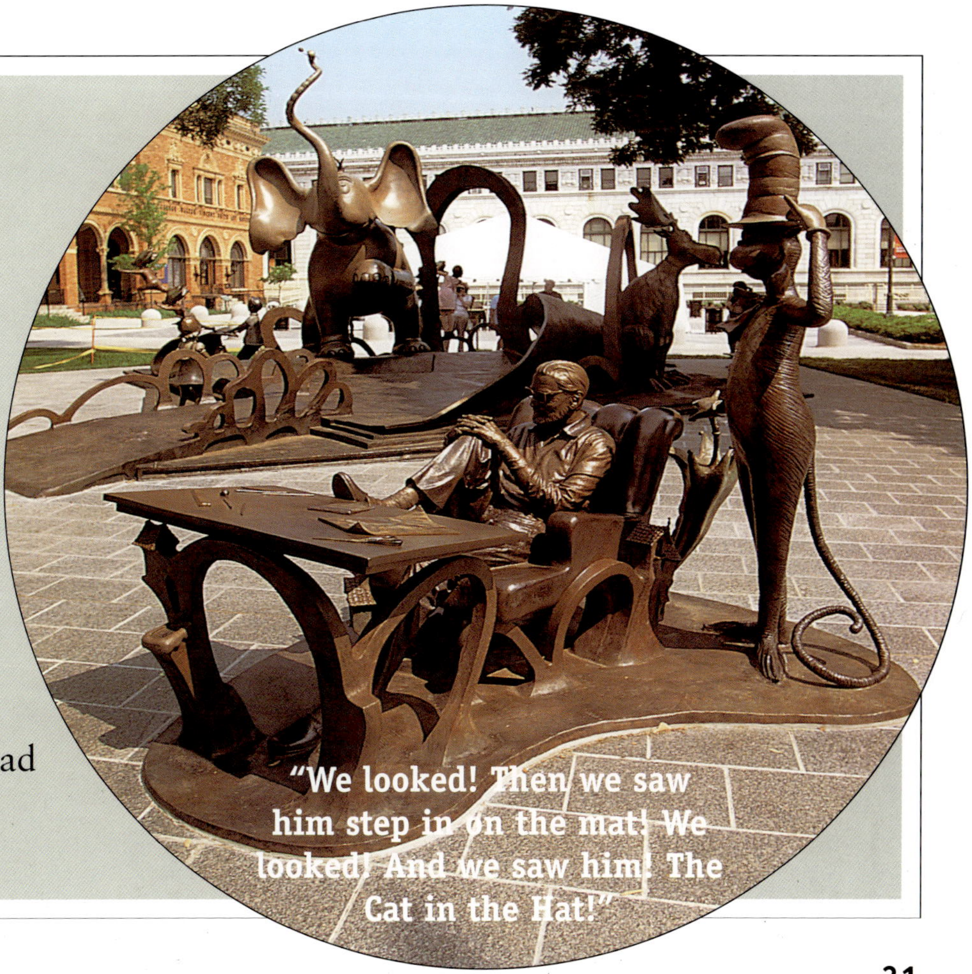

"We looked! Then we saw him step in on the mat! We looked! And we saw him! The Cat in the Hat!"

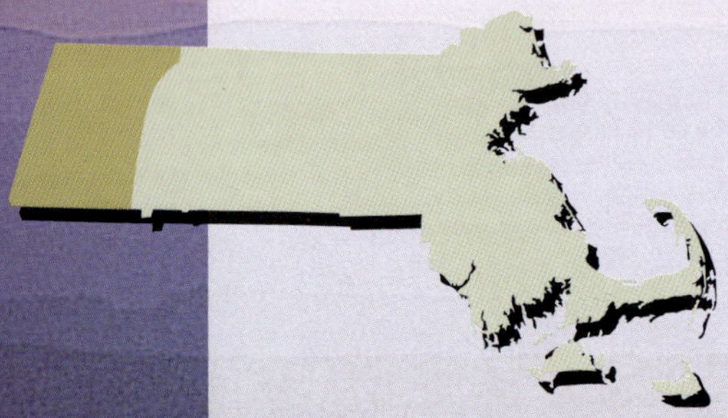

"Purple Hills"

We're climbing higher as the land begins to rise. We float toward the Berkshire Hills and Taconic Mountains. Can you see why people call them the purple hills? When the fog settles at dawn and dusk, the hills seem to turn purple.

Below us, dairy farms are tucked away along the Housatonic River. In the spring, the mountains bloom with dogwood trees and many colorful flowers. Our state flower, the mayflower, can be found here in spring. It is an ***endangered species*** in the rest of the state. That means there are not many of them left.

In the summer, the Berkshires come alive with the arts. People go to outdoor concerts at Tanglewood. Others go to festivals in Williamstown and Stockbridge.

More people come in the fall than at any other time of the year. The hills turn bright red, orange, and yellow as the leaves change. In the winter there is snow for skiers and snowshoers.

Is that an elk? A wolf? A bear? Even with all the tourists, you can sometimes catch a peek at these animals.

Home at Last

It has been an exciting ride. We've floated across our state and seen some beautiful places. We've looked down at some people who live, work, and play in Massachusetts. Our balloon is slowly drifting down to the ground. It is time to land and drive home. Now let's look at just where home is.

A Day at Butternut

Last winter my parents took me to Butternut so I could learn to ski. My parents love to ski, and they were sure I would too.

Mom got me a pair of mittens because they are warmer than gloves. I had to wear ski pants, because if you fall or sit on snow, it will melt, and you will get wet and cold if you don't have waterproof pants.

I don't have my own skis, so we went to the rental shop. There we found hundreds of skis, boots, and snowboards. It was really cold that day, so Mom got two heat packs, one for each boot. They looked like tea bags, and you put them inside the boots. At first the boots felt big and clumsy, but I got used to them.

I was in the Mountaineers class. The teachers showed us how to get our skis on. They showed us how to slide down the hill and how to stop. We side-stepped a little way up the hill and tried it.

Soon we were ready to try a lift. It looked like a moving walkway. We just walked our skis onto the belt and slowly it took us up the hill where we got off.

We learned to turn, first to one side and then to the other side. We practiced stopping.

Then the teacher told us that we were ready for the chairlift. There were people helping us get on the chair. They pulled down a safety bar. At the end of the fun ride, one of the teachers helped us off.

Before heading down the hill, we took off our skis and had lunch. Inside the Upper Lodge there is a special lunchroom for the Mountaineers.

When we came out, we had to find our skis and see if we remembered how to step into them again. We tapped the snow off before we tried to fit our boots into the bindings.

The teachers showed us how to ski a short way and stop. Soon we skied across the whole hill! We went farther and farther without stopping. At the end of the day, we could ski the whole hill and take the chairlift without help.

I could feel the wind in my face and the excitement of going fast. Soon I will be able to join mom and dad at the top of the mountain!

Memory Master

Lesson 2

1. What river is closest to where you live?
2. Name another river in Massachusetts.
3. Give an example of what the land is like in eastern Massachusetts.
4. Give an example of what the land is like in western Massachusetts.

Lesson 3

Your Home Town

PLACES TO LOCATE
Boston
New Bedford
Springfield
Your Town or City

WORDS TO UNDERSTAND
port
textile

Towns and Cities

We are part of New England. We live in Massachusetts. We also live in a city or town. Let's look closely at a few cities and towns around our state.

In the Spotlight: Boston

Boston is our capital city. It is where the leaders of our state meet to make laws. It is also the largest city in Massachusetts.

In Boston, you can ride the swan boats at the Public Garden, go to a Red Sox game, ice skate at Frog Pond, and ride the "T." There are tall buildings and busy streets. In other areas of the city, there are rows of brick homes called brownstones.

You can cross over the Charles River on several bridges. Crew teams row by on the water below. Ships come in and out of Boston Harbor.

Boston has many historic sites. You can follow the Freedom Trail around the city to see some of them. We will learn about the sites later in this book.

In the Spotlight: New Bedford

When most people think of New Bedford, they think of whaling. The ocean has played an important part in this town's history.

In the 1800s New Bedford was one of the world's greatest whaling **ports.** A port is a place where boats can dock. Sailors left New Bedford on ships. They sailed around the world hunting for whales. They brought back whale oil and bones to sell to other places.

Today, many people visit the New Bedford Whaling Museum. They can watch the boats on the water. They can sit on the beaches.

Many of New Bedford's people work in factories that make ***textiles*** (cloth), electrical machines, rubber products, and metal goods. The town has a large community of people whose ancestors came from Portugal.

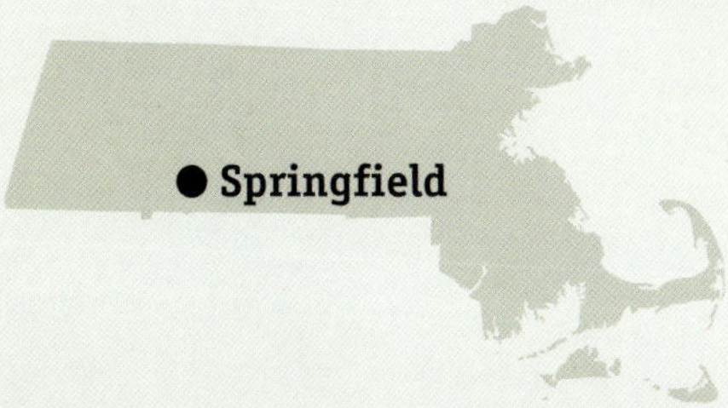

In the Spotlight: Springfield

The land around Springfield is different from the land around Boston and New Bedford. Springfield is in the Pioneer Valley. The Connecticut River flows right through the city. There are some tall buildings downtown, but you can see green rolling hills for miles and miles.

The people of Springfield are proud of their city. One reason is that the game of basketball was invented there many years ago. If you go there, you can visit the Basketball Hall of Fame.

Massachusetts

Activity

Using the Cardinal Directions, Scale, and Legend

Let's take a road trip! First climb in the car. Then use the cardinal directions, legend, and scale to answer the questions.

1. Find Boston on the map. What does the star by it mean?
2. Find Cape Ann. Which direction is Cape Ann from Boston?
3. You are in Brockton, and you want to go to Cape Cod. Which direction do you go first? ________ Then you go ________.
4. To drive from Boston to Worcester, you go _________.
5. The Connecticut River runs _________ and __________.
6. The Berkshires are _________ of the Connecticut River.
7. If you wanted to drive across Massachusetts from the western border to Boston, about how many miles would you travel?
8. If you wanted to drive from the New Hampshire border into Rhode Island, about how many miles would you have to travel?

Legend
Capital
Large City
Medium City
Small City
River
State Border
N
S
W
E
Amesbury
Salisbury
Newburyport
Haverhill
Rowley
Lawrence
Boxford
Ipswich
Pepperell
Merrimack River
Andover
Lowell
Topsfield
Essex
Cape Ann
Gloucester
Chelmsford
Ayer
Wilmington
Danvers
Beverly
Salem
Burlington
Woburn
Lynn
Massachusetts Bay
inton
Medford
Malden
Somerville
Waltham
Cambridge
Marlborough
Boston
Brookline
Framingham
Needham
Quincy
Milton
Hopkinton
Weymouth
North Scituate
Braintree
Norwood
Charles River
Milford
Holbrook
Marshfield Hills
Abington
Franklin
Brockton
Douglas
Green Harbor-Cedar Crest
Provincetown
Mansfield
Bridgewater
Kingston
Attleboro
Raynham Center
Plymouth
Taunton
Middleborough
CAPE COD BAY
Cape Cod
ATLANTIC OCEAN
North Eastham
Orleans
Brewster
Wareham
Buzzards Bay
Sagamore
Cape Cod Canal
Barnstable
Yarmouth Port
Chatham
Fall River
Mattapoisett
Centerville
Hyannis
Harwich
Rhode Island
New Bedford
Buzzards Bay
Woods Hole
Falmouth
Nantucket Sound
Vineyard Haven
Oak Bluffs
Edgartown
Rhode Island Sound
Martha's Vineyard
Nantucket
Nantucket
0
10
20
30
40
Scale of Miles

Activity

Describe Your Town

Where is your town? Find it on a map. Then answer these questions with your class:

1. Is your town in eastern Massachusetts, western Massachusetts, or somewhere in the middle?
2. What towns are close to yours?
3. Look out the window. What is the land around you like? Is it flat, rocky, or hilly? Are there beaches or woods nearby?
4. Is there a river or another waterway near your town? What direction is it from you?
5. Do you live in a city? Cities have tall buildings and busy streets. There are cars, trucks, and trains. People live close together in apartments. Do you live in a suburb? Suburbs are the areas just outside of the cities. They have more space and fewer people. They have houses and yards. Do you live in a small town in the country? Are there farms close to your home?
6. What do the people in your town do for a living? Can you think of some businesses in your town?
7. Do the adults you know work in your town, or do they go to another town or city to work?
8. Does your town have a library? Does it have a historical society? Find out where they are located.

A Look Ahead

In this chapter, we learned about the land called New England. We learned about the land called Massachusetts. You learned about the land in your town. Now we will learn about these places by reading about the people who have lived here in the past. We will see how they made history.

Lesson 3

Memory Master

1. Tell something you know about another town in Massachusetts.
2. Describe the land in your town.

Chapter 2 Review

What's the Point?

Massachusetts is part of a larger area called New England. It has rolling hills, forests, rocky coasts, sandy beaches, and lots of rivers. It has cities, towns, and farms. It is home to people from many different backgrounds.

When people think of Massachusetts, they think of things such as fall leaves, maple syrup, lobsters and clams, and great colleges. What do people think of when they think of your town?

Activity

Literature Tie-In

Write About a Personal Experience

Do you like living in Massachusetts? Can you remember a time when you felt proud of our state or your hometown?

Think about some experiences you have had in Massachusetts. Maybe you and your family went to the Cape for a vacation. Maybe you like to jump into a huge pile of leaves in the fall, or watch the snow fall outside the window.

Write a story, poem, or skit about your life in Massachusetts. Or make a poster showing things you like to do.

Activity

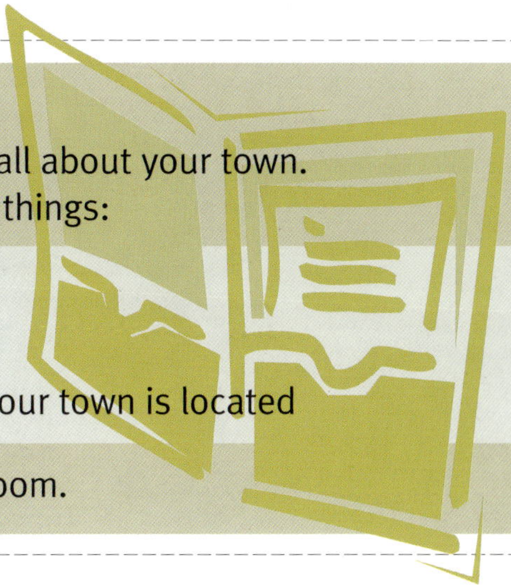

Make a Brochure

Pretend someone is coming to visit, and you want to tell him or her all about your town. Make a brochure about your town. Create a page to show each of these things:

- the land and/or water
- plants and animals
- things to do
- different kinds of homes
- the jobs people do
- a map that shows where your town is located

Put all the pages together. Hang everyone's brochures around the room.

Native Americans were the first people to live here. This woman shows how they planted crops long ago. Look at her clothing. Now look at the ground around her. What season do you think it is?

Chapter 3

The First People

"As I set out for the forest, the sun is rising. It has not warmed the ground yet, and the birds are just beginning to sing. I say prayers to our Creator . . . and to the spirits of the animals. I ask for success in hunting today. . . . I am eager to bring back a good catch to my mother."

—*from* Tapenum's Day
by Kate Waters

Lesson 1

The First People of Massachusetts

WORDS TO UNDERSTAND
native
tribe

Go Back in Time

Close your eyes for a minute. Go back in time. Go back hundreds of years, before any settlers came across the ocean to Massachusetts. There are no cars or highways. There are no airplanes flying in the sky. There are no stores or office buildings.

All around you are forests. You can smell the ocean close by. What sounds do you hear? You might see a line of smoke rising from the trees. If you follow the smoke, you might find people cooking food over a fire.

The people are dressed in soft deerskins and animal furs. Who are they? They call themselves the Wampanoag [womp u NUCK]. That name means "people of the first light," or "people of the dawn."

Today we call the Wampanoag and other tribes Native Americans. ***Native*** means they were the first people to live here. Native Americans have lived here for thousands of years.

Find the Wampanoag lands. What other tribes lived in what is now Massachusetts? Which tribes lived closest to where you live today?

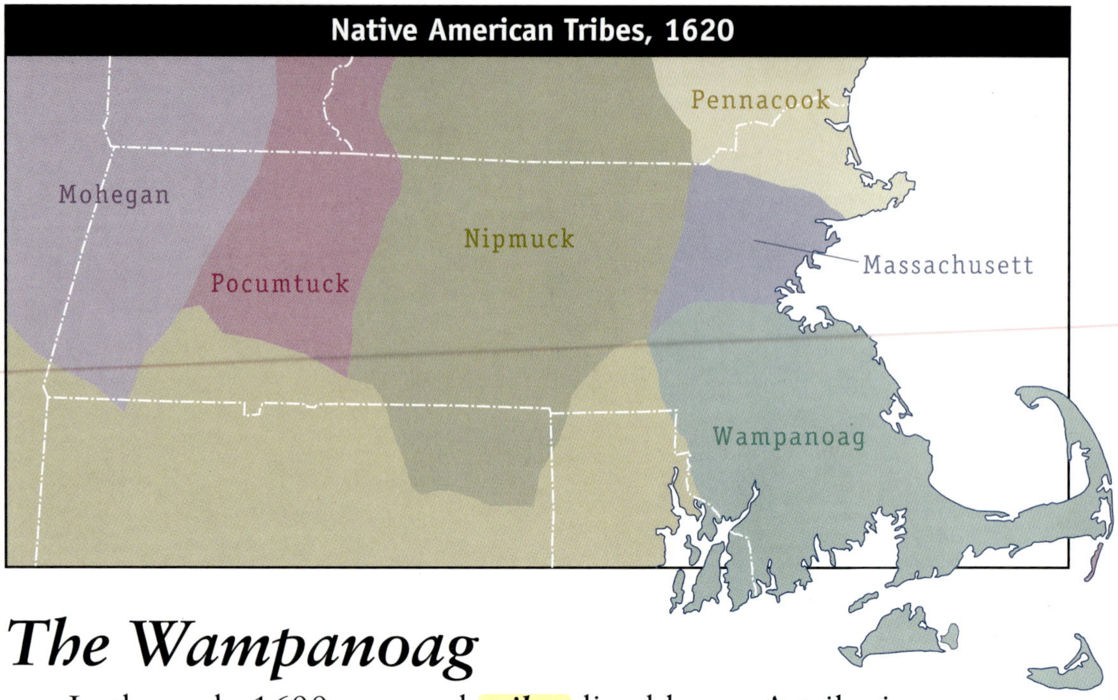

The Wampanoag

In the early 1600s, several ***tribes*** lived here. A tribe is a community of Native Americans. The tribes shared the land we call Massachusetts. The Wampanoag tribe was one of these. We will focus on their way of life in this chapter. The other tribes may have done things a bit differently.

On Wampanoag land there were many villages. There were paths from village to village. The people in the villages spoke the same language. Look at the map to see where the Wampanoag lived.

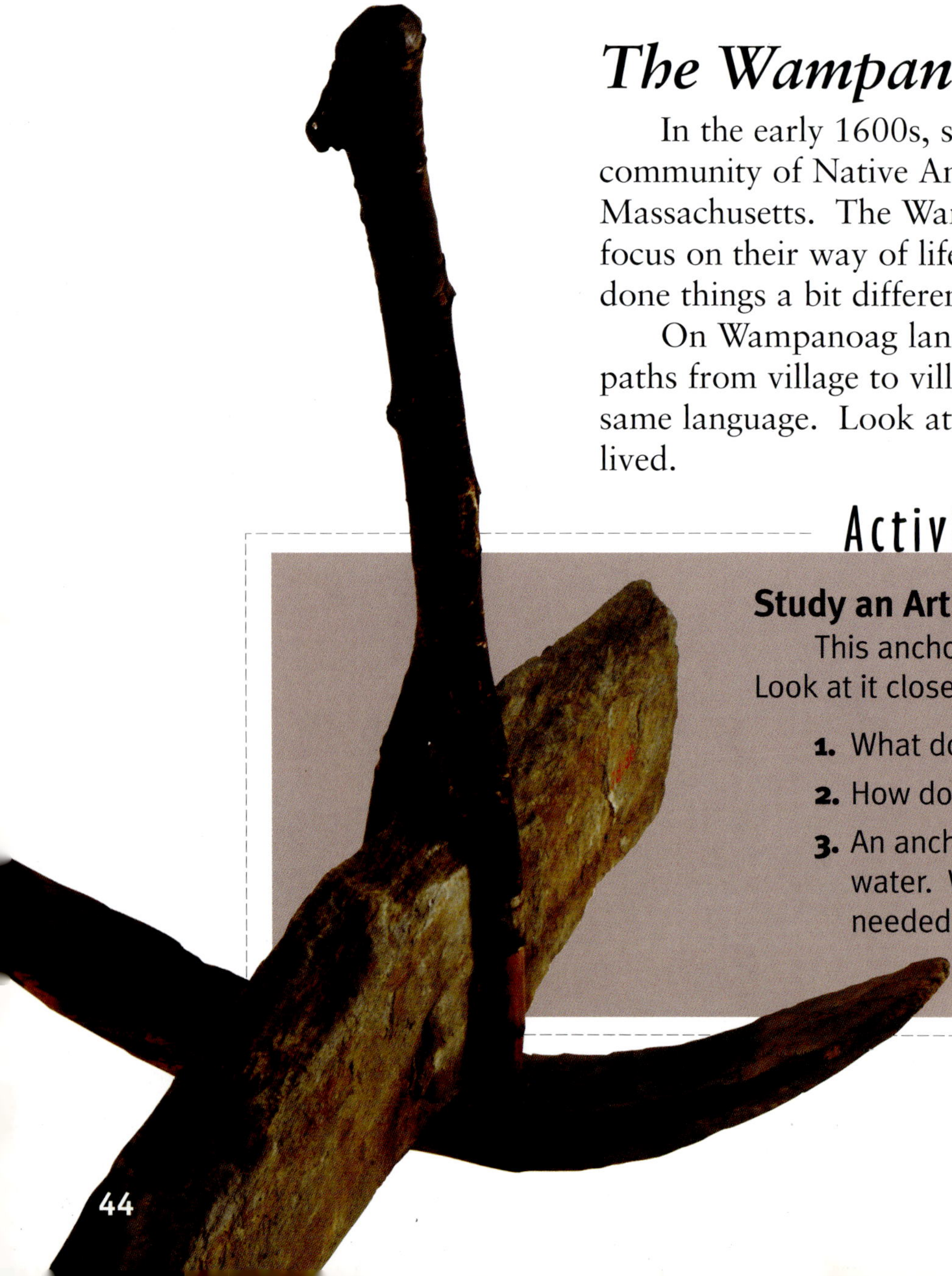

Activity

Study an Artifact

This anchor was made by Native Americans long ago. Look at it closely, and answer the questions.

1. What do you think the anchor was made of?
2. How do you think the people made it?
3. An anchor is used to hold a boat in place in the water. Why do you think the people might have needed an anchor?

▲ Courtesy of The Peabody Museum

Activity

Compare Maps

Study the maps, and answer the questions.

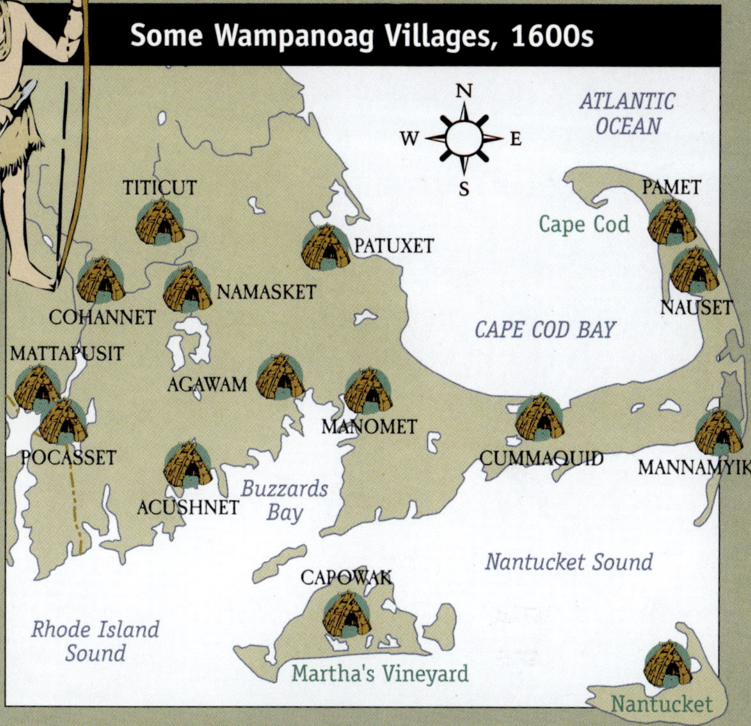

1. Look at the title of the map on the left. What does this map show?
2. What does the map on the right show?
3. Name the village that once stood where Wellfleet is today.
4. What modern town was once called Patuxet?

Memory Master

Lesson 1

1. What is a tribe?
2. Name one tribe that lived in the land we call Massachusetts.
3. What does the name *Wampanoag* mean?

Lesson 2

Everyday Life

WORDS TO UNDERSTAND

cattail
cradleboard
gourd
harvest
longhouse
mishoon
patient
respect
sapling
sinew
tan
wetu

Living With the Land

The people got everything they needed from nature. There was soil for planting crops. The forests gave them animals to hunt. The ocean and rivers gave them water for fishing, drinking, cooking, washing, and traveling.

If you were a young Wampanoag boy or girl, your life followed the seasons. Let's read about some of the things you would do in the spring, summer, fall, and winter.

Spring and Summer by the Sea

In the spring and summer, you live near the seashore. Your family has a planting ground there.

The year begins when the herring move up the river to lay their eggs. A herring is a small fish. Your family catches so many herring—how will you eat them all? You smoke the extra fish so they will last a long time without going bad.

These men are catching eels. Can you see the special trap they made?

The men get the land ready for planting. Your father and the other men cut down trees. First they put mud or clay part way up the trunks. Then they light a fire around the trunks. The fire cuts through the trunks but stops at the mud. The men scrape away the ashes. Soon the trees fall to the ground. Later, the men use the fallen trees to make boats, or ***mishoons.***

Once the land is clear, your mother plants corn, beans, and squash. Your father grows tobacco in another field.

Your mother also digs for clams and finds lobsters in the surf. She finds nuts, roots, and berries to eat. She gathers plants for medicine. She collects grasses to weave into baskets. Your father catches fish and eels from the ocean and rivers.

The wild strawberries are ripe! You pick mounds of them. Your family celebrates with songs and dances.

The "three sisters"—corn, beans, and squash—were planted close together. The beans climbed up the cornstalks as they grew.

Older children helped guard the crops. They scared away birds that came to eat the corn.

The Amazing Cranberry

Cranberries grew on the wet land. They were an important food. Native Americans said that cranberries were sent to them from the Great Spirit. He knew his people needed a good supply of food. He sent a dove carrying the first cranberries to the people.

A Summer Home

Your family makes a home called a ***wetu.*** They use wood, bark, and grasses to build the wetu.

Your father and the other men make the frame out of young trees that bend. These are called ***saplings.*** The people dig holes to hold the saplings in place. They bend the saplings over and tie them together with vines or animal skins. They cover the frame with bark or mats made from grasses. They leave a door and a hole in the top so the smoke from the fire can escape.

Spring is the only time to find saplings. Your family collects enough for the wetu, plus more to save for your winter home.

Spring is also the time to peel bark from the trees. Your family uses some of the bark for the wetu and saves the rest to cover your winter home.

▲ Photo by John Alley

A Step-by-Step Wetu

1

To build a wetu, the people cut down saplings. They trimmed off the branches. Then they dug holes in the ground. They put saplings in the holes. This held the saplings in place.

2 *The people bent the saplings over, then lashed them together with cord, vines, or animals skins. This made a frame.*

3 *They covered the frame with bark or mats made of grasses and reeds. They left a door. They also left a hole in the top so smoke from the fire could escape.*

Fall and Winter in the Forest

In the fall your mother ***harvests*** the crops. She dries some of the vegetables to save them for winter.

Your father watches the sky for signs that winter is coming. When winter is close, you get ready to move away from the shore and into the forest. Your father digs a deep hole in the earth. He leaves bags of dried food in the hole. He makes sure the hole is deep enough that animals won't dig up the food.

Your mother unties the ***cattail*** mats and asks you to roll them up. They are not heavy, so you can carry them to the winter village. Your mother carries your baby sister on her back in a ***cradleboard.***

Winter Homes

Your family joins relatives as they return to the winter village. Your father and the other men take out the saplings and bark they saved from the spring. They make a ***longhouse.*** You share the longhouse with cousins, aunts, and uncles. You are happy to be with them and tell them what you did all summer.

Your mother uses the mats to line the inside walls of the longhouse. This helps keep everyone warm. It also helps you know where your family will be in the longhouse.

A longhouse is like a wetu but larger and longer. The longhouse was a busy place.

Inside the longhouse, each family has a fire for cooking. There is not a lot of furniture because the house is mostly used for sleeping. You spend most of your time outdoors. Beds line the walls around the entire house. You have piles of furs to keep you warm. There is always food on one of the cooking fires.

Above each fire is a hole in the roof. The smoke goes out through the holes. When it rains or snows, you move a mat or piece of bark across part of the hole. That way the smoke can still get out, but the rain or snow cannot get in.

Your father and the other men build a smokehouse. That's where they smoke meat to make it last longer.

A Time for Hunting

Your father hunts deer, bears, squirrels, and raccoons. He has to be fast to follow the animals and strong to carry them home. He also has to be ***patient*** and quiet to hide in the forest. When there is ice on the pond, he makes a hole in it so he can fish with a spear. You eat fresh meat every day. You smoke the rest so you can eat it later.

You bundle up in blankets made of fur from deer, raccoons, and beavers. You sit by the warm fire. You listen to your grandparents tell stories.

"These are more than stories, you know. They are the heart of our culture."
—Manitonquat

Telling History Through Stories

It is winter, and you are tired of being inside. Your grandmother puts a few more sticks on the fire. She tells you and your brothers and sisters to come and sit around the fire.

She begins to tell you a story about how Martha's Vineyard and Nantucket came to be. A giant named Moshop had something to do with it. You listen closely. Someday you will tell this story to your children.

Moshop was so big that he used Cape Cod as his bed. One night he had bad dreams. As he tossed and turned, his moccasins filled with sand. He emptied his moccasins, one at a time, a short way out to sea. One pile of sand became the island of *Noepe*, or Martha's Vineyard. The other made the island of *Natockete*, or Nantucket.

Making Clothing

Today we buy clothes, tools, and toys at a store. If you were a Wampanoag child in the 1600s, your family made these things.

Native Americans used almost every part of the animals they hunted. Let's say your father brings home a deer or moose. Your mother cooks the meat for dinner. You use the skin for clothing and blankets. How does your mother sew the clothes? She uses the bones as needles and the ***sinews,*** or tendons, as thread. An animal bladder makes a great bag for carrying things.

In the summer you wear an apron, or breechcloth, and a belt around your waist if you are a boy. If you are a girl you wear a skirt. It is made of animal skin. Your mother ***tans*** the skin, or stretches it to make it lighter. You go barefoot. You wear a deerskin pouch so you can carry things with you.

In the winter you wear warm leggings with fur inside. You wrap a blanket or warm robe around your shoulders. Your mother makes them from the skins of seals, black bears, raccoons, river otters, foxes, squirrels, beavers, muskrats, or wolves. You put on moccasins to keep your feet warm.

Sometimes you wear jewelry made of bone, shell, stone, claws, or antlers.

Which man is dressed for winter? Which man is dressed for summer? Describe some of the things the men are wearing. How do you think these things were made?

Making Tools

Men made their own boats, or mishoons. *They burned the center of a tree trunk and scraped out the dead wood. They used the boats to travel on the rivers and in the ocean.*

Your mother makes pots out of clay. Then she uses the fire to make them hard and strong. She uses the pots for cooking. She makes a stew with roast corn and deer meat. She puts the pot over the fire in the morning and cooks the stew all day long. She adds more meat and vegetables to it as it gets eaten. Sometimes she makes bread from ground corn. Your mother also makes baskets out of grasses or bark. She uses baskets to carry squash and beans from the garden.

Your father carves stone and wood into tools. He and the other men make bows, arrows, animal traps, hooks, spears, canoes, and bowls. He makes axes by burning a hole in a piece of wood and setting a stone in the hole.

Your family makes rattles and drums so you can make music. You put seeds inside a dried ***gourd.*** Then you plug the end with a corncob. When you shake the gourd, you can hear the seeds rattle.

The Children Learn

You and all the children learn skills that will help you survive. Everyone works to help the family.

If you are a boy, you learn all about the woods, rivers, and ocean. You learn how to look for animal tracks. You learn how to tell rabbit tracks from turkey tracks. You try to be very quiet in the forest. You listen and watch for animals.

You sharpen arrows and practice your aim. You run so you can get faster and faster. You watch the men make tools so you can make your own someday. You find wood for the fire. Maybe you dream about becoming a leader or warrior when you grow up.

If you are a girl, you learn all about working in the fields and garden. You learn which wild plants you can eat. You learn to cook over the fire. You learn to take care of children. You help your mother dig for clams and clay. When you are old enough, you will learn how to sew clothes.

Time To Play

There is time to play, so you and your friends splash in the river or pond. You roam the fields together. You dance and sing. You play Hubbub. Hubbub is a game like dice, played with shells or painted stones. You also play a game like football. The ball is made of deer skin and stuffed with fur. You have races and bow-and-arrow contests. It is fun when the whole village has a special feast.

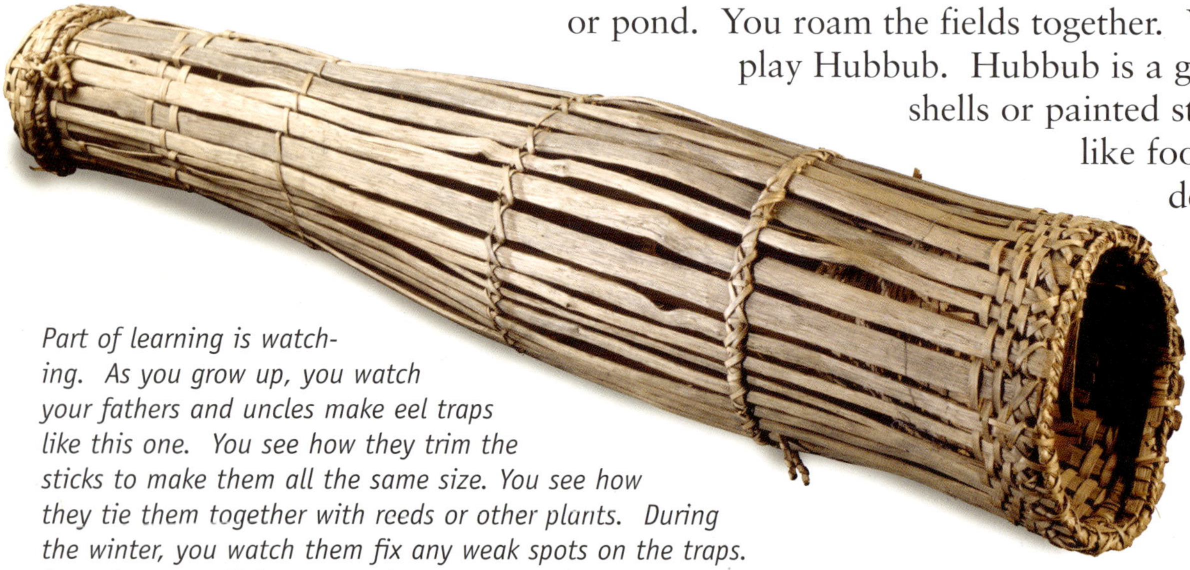

Part of learning is watching. As you grow up, you watch your fathers and uncles make eel traps like this one. You see how they trim the sticks to make them all the same size. You see how they tie them together with reeds or other plants. During the winter, you watch them fix any weak spots on the traps. Someday you will have to make your own eel trap.

◄ Courtesy of The Peabody Museum

A Spiritual World

Like all people, the Native Americans had—and still have—beliefs about how life began. They had beliefs about what happens to us after we die. There were rules about how to treat one another—not just people, but plants and animals too.

The Wampanoag understood that they were one small piece of a big puzzle. Without one piece, the puzzle was never complete. If one piece was in the wrong place, the other pieces would not fit.

The people said that when the Creator made the world, he gave instructions to all the living things. The instructions were very important to follow. For the people, the instructions were to protect the land. This is why families lived in one place for no more than ten years at a time. They knew the land needed to rest from all that was taken during that time.

Respect for Living Things

The Wampanoag believed life was given to all things. It should be treated with ***respect.*** The people had ways of saying thank you every day. When men cut down a tree, they offered thanks to the tree for giving its life. When they killed an animal, they thanked the animal. When the herring came in spring, they sang and danced. When it was time to pick strawberries, they danced and played games.

They prayed by dancing and singing. In the spring, they thanked the Great Spirit for taking away winter and bringing warmth back to the land. In the summer, they got together for the Green Corn Dance. They thanked the Great Spirit for their crops. After the harvest, they had a great feast of thanksgiving. They ate as much food as they could. They asked the Great Spirit to protect them in the long winter months ahead.

Memory Master

Lesson 2

1. Describe how the people made their homes.
2. List two ways the people got food.
3. Describe some of the chores a boy or girl did.
4. Give an example of how the people treated nature with respect.

Lesson 3

Leaders, Trade, and War

WORDS TO UNDERSTAND
council
pniese
powwow
sachem
trade
wampum

Leading the Tribe

Every tribe had a leader, or ***sachem*** [SAY chum]. The sachem could be a man or a woman. It was the sachem's job to keep the community happy. The sachem was also in charge of resources on the tribe's land.

Only a sachem was allowed to wear a black wolf skin. Many people gave him gifts of small beads made from clam shells. These beads are called ***wampum.*** People gave wampum when they thought the sachem was being a good leader.

Wampum was made into belts. The pictures on the belts showed the tribe's history. Often, sachems gathered all the people in the village to hear the stories. They did not want the stories to be forgotten.

The sachem had helpers, called the ***council.*** The people on the council were older. They were wise from the many years they had walked the Earth. A ***pniese*** [p'neece] was often part of the council. A *pniese* was a great warrior. He helped the sachem decide how to go to battle or how to stay out of a battle. The Wampanoag sometimes fought wars against other tribes.

The sachem also had help from the medicine man or woman. The medicine person knew what plants could be used to heal the sick. He knew songs or dances for healing. Only a medicine person was allowed to wear antlers on top of his head.

What things in this picture tell you this man might be a leader or a person on the council?

▲ Photo ©Kindra Clineff

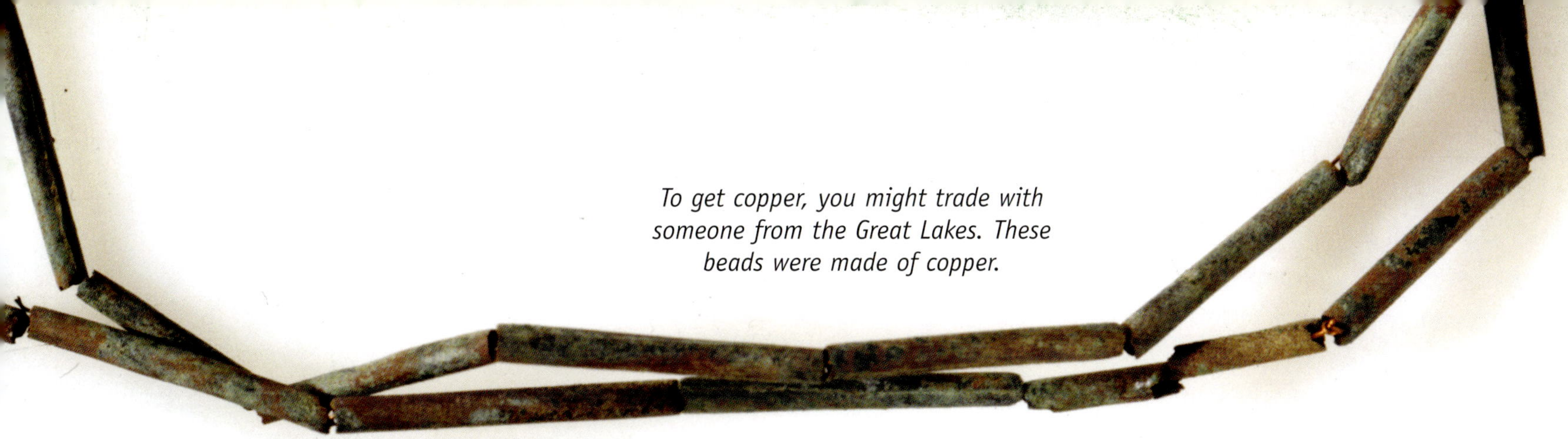

To get copper, you might trade with someone from the Great Lakes. These beads were made of copper.

Trade

The Wampanoag people ***traded*** with people from other tribes. Let's say your tribe had a lot of wooden bowls and corn seed. You did not have stone that was good for making pipes. You did not have copper pots. Tribes from other places had these things. How could you get them? You could trade for them. You could give them your bowls, and they could give you their copper.

To get to other places, you followed trails through the woods. Then you paddled canoes along the rivers or down the coast. It was a long journey.

When visitors came to a village, the people offered them food. It was a way of saying, "Let's be friends."

Change on the Way

It seemed that life would go on like this forever. In the spring, the people would return to their planting sites. In the summer, they would grow corn, beans, and squash. They would harvest their crops in fall and return to their village for winter. The men, women, and children would all work together to make sure everyone had a good life. The Great Spirit would watch over them and protect them from harm.

But a big change was coming. In the 1600s, sailors and fishermen started to come from across the ocean. Soon after, people settled on Wampanoag land. More and more people came and took more land. In time, Native Americans and their leaders faced hard times. The circle of life that held them together started to come undone.

To get flint or soapstone for pipes, you might trade with someone from the South.

◂ *The people made wampum out of quahoag shells. They used tools to shape the beads and drill tiny holes in them. Then they strung them together and made belts or necklaces.*

In October, the Aquinnah Wampanoag celebrate Cranberry Day. They gather to thank the Creator for a good harvest. They pick cranberries, tell stories, dance, and drum. Children learn history by doing tasks that people long ago did. They have a big supper in the evening.

The Wampanoag Today

The Wampanoag are not just people of the past. Some tribes still live in Massachusetts. The Mashpee Wampanoag live on Cape Cod. The Aquinnah Wampanoag live on Martha's Vineyard. Their ancestors are the people you just read about.

The men, women, and children are proud of their history on this land. They try to keep their way of life. They learn the stories of those who came before them.

Technology Tie-In

As a class, learn about other Native American groups living in modern Massachusetts. Some tribes have websites. Visit these websites, and make a calendar of Native American events around the state.

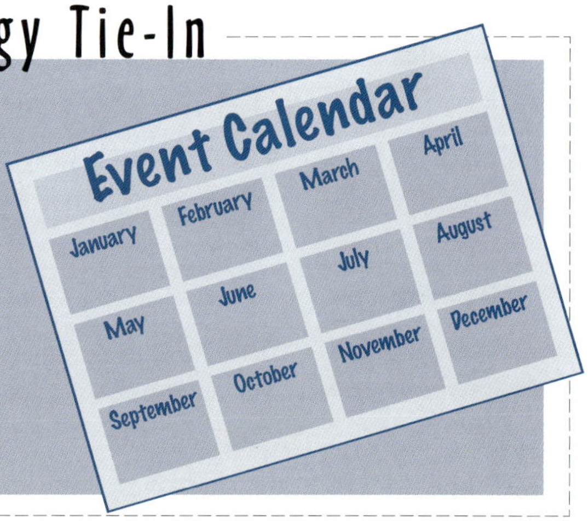

Lesson 3

Memory Master

1. The leader of the tribe was called the _______.
2. Give an example of a trade.
3. How did people travel to trade with other tribes?
4. Name one thing modern Native Americans do to keep their history alive.

Each year on the Fourth of July weekend, the Mashpee Wampanoag have a **powwow.** *They share their food, crafts, songs, and dances for three days.*

Chapter 3 Review

What's the Point?

Native Americans were the first people to live in the land we call Massachusetts. They got food by hunting, fishing, and planting crops. They used what they found in nature to cook meals, build homes, and make tools. Adults taught the children skills and told them their history through stories. Many of their descendants live in our state today. They work hard to keep their history alive.

Geography Tie-In

Native Americans were the first to name many places in Massachusetts. Here are some of the names and what they mean:

Agawam = land beneath water
Chappaquiddick = separate island
Chicopee = rapids
Housatonic = area beyond the mountain
Nantasket = there it is grassy
Nantucket = tidal run around sharp angle
Manomet = at the look-out place
Mashpee = the greater cove
Merrimack (River) = between land
Menemsha = between sea
Swampscott = at the red rock

1. As a class, find some of these places on a map of Massachusetts.
2. Discuss why you think the people gave the places these names.
3. In small groups, think about the name of your town. What new name could you give your town that describes the land or what you see there?

Literature Tie-In

Write a Story

Go back and look at pages 42 and 43. Now that you have read about daily life for the Wampanoag, what do you see in this drawing? What does it show about how the people lived?

Use the picture to help you imagine life as a Wampanoag boy or girl long ago. Then write a story, play, or song about one day or event. What was happening in the village? What did you see, hear, and smell around you? Draw a picture to go with your story.

In many tribes, people had spirit guides. The spirit guide, or *manito*, guarded a person for life. It was a very special, sacred thing. Here is a story about a boy who went on a special journey to find his *manito*.

Read the story, and answer the questions below.

In Search of a Manito

It was the boy's third night away from home. As darkness fell, he wondered if he was ready for his test after all. He was very hungry, tired, and lonely.

He thought back to the day he had left home. His mother had made his favorite meal—corn cakes with wild blueberries. But later, she scolded him and told him to leave. He knew parents sometimes did this as a signal. It was a signal that his searching time had come.

For two days he had walked in the woods, looking for signs that might tell him who or what his spirit guide was. But he had found nothing but an old fish hook made of bone and a wolf's tooth. He placed them in the little leather pouch he had made.

He found himself drawn to the big river a few miles from camp. He waded out to a favorite spot, a huge rock. There he rested. He ran his fingers over the pictures someone had carved in the rock many years ago. This made him feel better, for now he didn't feel so alone. Soon, the gentle lapping of the river against the rock made him fall asleep.

And then he had a strange dream. He was down at the river fishing, but nothing would bite. A starving wolf sneaked up on him. It was ready to attack. Just as the boy saw the wolf and turned to run, a huge catfish jumped from the water and onto the bank. The wolf looked from the boy to the fish. In a split second, the wolf grabbed the fish and ran away.

When the boy woke up, he remembered his strange dream. Just then a swish in the water made him look down. In the dim morning light, he saw a huge catfish swimming at his feet. Slowly and gently, he put his hand into the water. When the fish didn't move, he stroked it lightly. Then it turned and swam away.

The boy jumped up and down. "You. It is you!" he cried to the fish. "You are my *manito*, my spirit guide and protector." He was so happy. And now he knew that the fish hook and wolf's tooth in his pouch were important after all!

The boy ran home, holding tight to his leather pouch. He wanted to find his father and tell him about his dream.

Adapted from a story by Terry Baker

1. Why was the boy away from home alone?
2. What animal became his spirit guide?
3. In the dream, how did his spirit guide protect him?
4. Do you think things were different when the boy went back home? Why or why not?

The Pilgrims

There was a ship, Mayflower by name; Hey, Ho~
Took a trip, she crossed the main; Hey, Ho~
Full of people seeking peace,
Praying for freedom to increase;
Hey, Ho, Dee-o, Dee-o!

The Pilgrims came to Plymouth Rock; Hey, Ho~
Simple people, sturdy stock; Hey, Ho~
To be free they crossed the sea,
Thanked the Lord on bended knee;
Hey, Ho, Dee-o, Dee-o!

How when the crops were gathered in; Hey, Ho~
A dinner party did begin; Hey, Ho~
Pilgrims, Indians, pumpkin pie,
Turkey, venison, corn, oh my!
Hey, Ho, Dee-o, Dee-o!

—from "Ballad of the Mayflower"
By Linda G. Paulsen

Chapter 4

A group of men, women, and children called the Pilgrims came to America on a ship called the Mayflower. *They started Plimoth Colony.*

Pretend you are on the deck of the Mayflower. *The anchor is down, but the sails flap in the cold wind. It has been a long, hard trip across the ocean. You are tired of the rocking ship and its creaky boards. As you look out at the shore, you wonder what your new life will be like in this land.*

Lesson 1

The Pilgrims

PEOPLE TO KNOW
Dorothy Bradford
William Bradford

PLACES TO LOCATE
England
Holland (the Netherlands)
America
Virginia
Provincetown
Plimoth (Plymouth)

WORDS TO UNDERSTAND
colony
govern
government
governor
meetinghouse
printing press
scarce
scurvy
self-government

Who Were the Pilgrims?

It is time to close your eyes again. This time, pretend you are in England. Go back about 400 years. It is the early 1600s.

Your family is unhappy. You are not free to live the way you want to live. The king says you must belong to his church. You can't belong to your own church. If you do, you will go to jail. This is what happened to a group of people called the Pilgrims.

The Pilgrims talked about what to do. They wanted to find a place where they could worship in their own church. They decided to leave England. Where could they go?

First, the Pilgrims sailed to Holland. But this led to more problems. They decided to start a new life across the ocean in America. They would go and join other English people who had settled in a place called Virginia.

What do you think?

Do you think your family would move far away in order to worship the way they wanted?

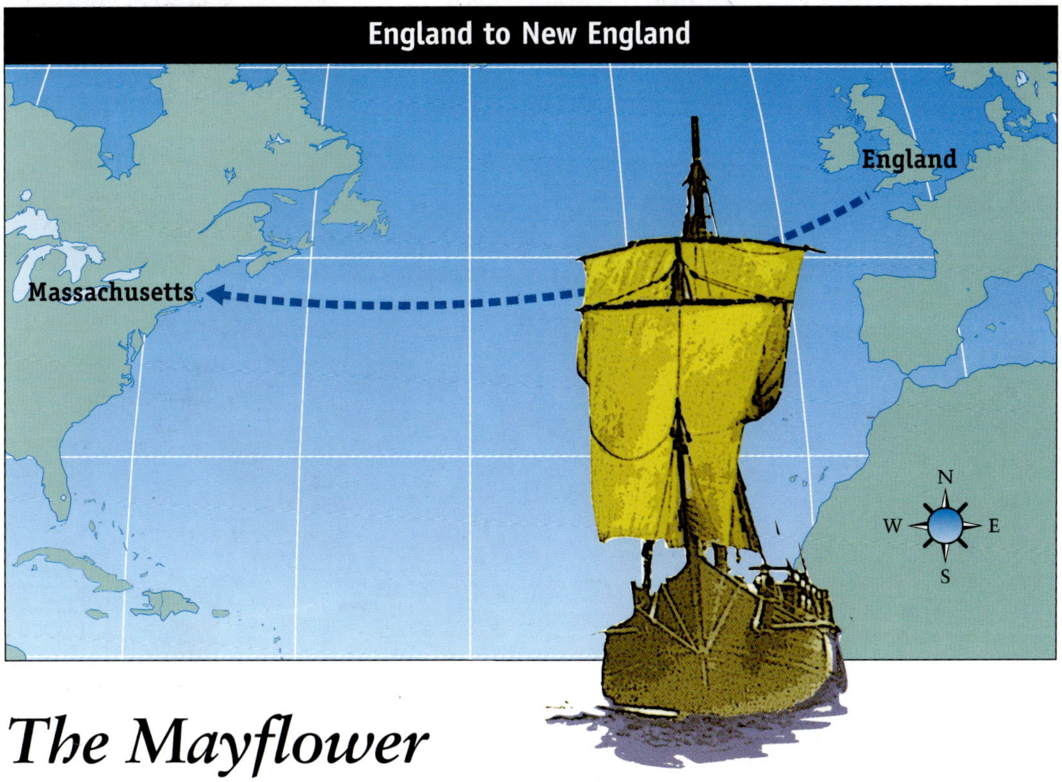

The Mayflower

After saying goodbye to their loved ones, the Pilgrims boarded a ship called the *Mayflower*. They began a very long journey.

The trip across the ocean was rough. For two months, the *Mayflower* rolled and pitched along. The little ship ran into icy winds and high waves. Many people got sick during the terrible storms.

One night a piece of wood that helped to hold the ship together cracked in two! Luckily the crew was able to prop it back up. They used a ***printing press*** they had on board to do this. The ship sailed on.

Even though the trip to America was very hard, only two people died. One was a sailor and one was a servant. One baby was born on the ship. His parents named him Oceanus.

Finally, one morning the crew saw land. But it was not Virginia. It was the sandy banks of Cape Cod.

The *Speedwell*

You've probably heard of the *Mayflower* before. But have you heard of the *Speedwell*? It was another ship that carried Pilgrims. It soon began to leak, so everyone got on the *Mayflower*.

Math Tie-In

How many people were on the *Mayflower*? There were 41 Pilgrims, including 14 children. There were also 61 other people. Some were soldiers like Myles Standish. Some were craftsmen like John Alden. Others were sailors, of course.

You do the math. How many total people were on board?

Inside the Mayflower

If you think the voyage on the *Mayflower* was fun, think again! Here is how one writer described it:

> *The ship is small, wet, and foul. The smells are horrid. There is no place to change or wash clothes. Each adult [has] a space below deck measuring seven by two and a half feet. Children get even less room. None of the passengers is allowed on deck; there is little fresh air below and many are sick. Fresh food soon runs out and then there is hard bread and dried meat that is wet and moldy. But the Pilgrims have onions, lemon juice, and beer to keep them from getting . . . **scurvy**.*
>
> —*Joy Hakim*

With a ruler or yardstick, measure seven feet long and two and a half feet wide on the floor. Mark the space with yarn. That is how much room each person had below deck. Can you see why the people wanted to go up on deck?

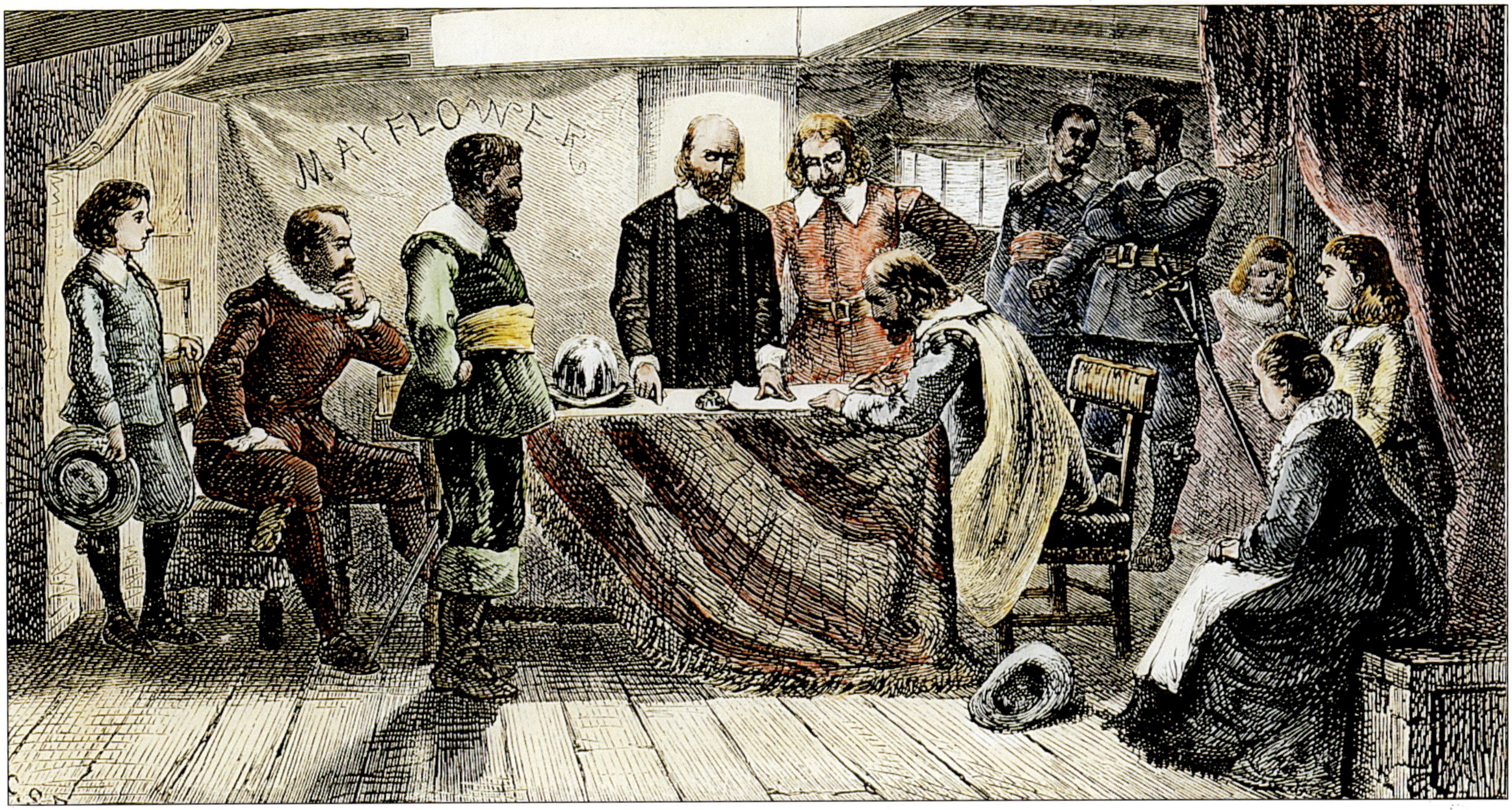

The Pilgrims made history when they signed the Mayflower Compact.

The Mayflower Compact

The Pilgrims wanted to make some rules before anyone went ashore. They were far from England and alone in the wilderness. They would have to **govern,** or make the rules, themselves.

They wrote a paper called the Mayflower Compact. It was a promise that they would work together to make good laws for their new home. All the men signed it.

Here are the main ideas of the Mayflower Compact:

- We made this journey for the glory of God; our country, England; and our King, James I.
- We planned to settle in the northern part of Virginia, but we are now in Massachusetts.
- In the presence of God and one another, we promise to form a **government** for our new colony.
- All of us will obey the laws of our new government.

The moment the Pilgrims signed the Mayflower Compact was a very important one in our country's history. A free people had made their own plan of government. They agreed to live together under laws they would make. This is called **self-government.**

A **colony** is a settlement in another country far away.

Massachusetts PORTRAIT

William Bradford
1590–1657

William Bradford was a leader of the Pilgrims. He was born in England.

As William grew, he felt very strongly about religion. He did not like the king's church. He and a group of others wanted to do things differently. They moved to Holland and called themselves "Pilgrims."

When the Pilgrims decided to go to America, William planned the trip. He helped get the money and the ship. He and his wife, Dorothy, sailed on the *Mayflower*. When the Pilgrims got to Massachusetts, Dorothy fell off the ship and drowned. Later, William married Alice Southworth. They had three children together.

William kept notes and wrote in his diary. He wrote about the trip across the ocean. He made a copy of the Mayflower Compact. He wrote about the first winter the Pilgrims spent in their new home. He wrote about the hard work it took to start the colony. Later, he used his notes to write a book about the colony.

The Pilgrims chose William Bradford to be their ***governor*** (after the first governor died). He was chosen again and again because he did a good job. He did his best to help the Pilgrims stick to their goals.

Going Ashore

The Pilgrims went ashore at what is now Provincetown. They fell on their knees and thanked God for getting them safely across the ocean. They looked back out to sea and saw whales swimming off shore. They then looked at the miles of empty sand dunes stretching along Cape Cod.

William Bradford was there. He wrote about the Pilgrims' feelings:

> *They now had no friends to welcome them . . . nor houses or much less towns to [go] to . . . it was winter, and they that know the winters of that country know them to be sharp and violent . . . besides what could they see but a . . . wilderness before them, . . . if they looked behind them, there was the mighty ocean which they had passed!*

The Pilgrims looked for the best place to settle. The winds grew colder all the time. Snow fell on the deck of the *Mayflower*.

The men went ashore to hunt and explore. Sometimes they saw Native people who fled as they came near. At other times, they were met with arrows. The women went ashore to wash the clothes. For the rest of the winter, they stayed on the ship with the children.

What do you think?

Can you imagine what the Wampanoag people thought when they first saw the Pilgrims coming ashore? What would you have thought if people who looked very different from anyone you had ever seen before started to bring their things ashore?

The Pilgrims Choose Plimoth

The Pilgrims finally chose a place to build a colony. It was a place Captain John Smith had called Plimoth. (Today we spell it Plymouth.)

It seemed like a good place to settle. There was a spring of fresh water nearby. A high hill ran down to the ocean. It gave a clear view of any ships that might be coming. There were cherry and plum trees. When summer came, the trees would give fruit.

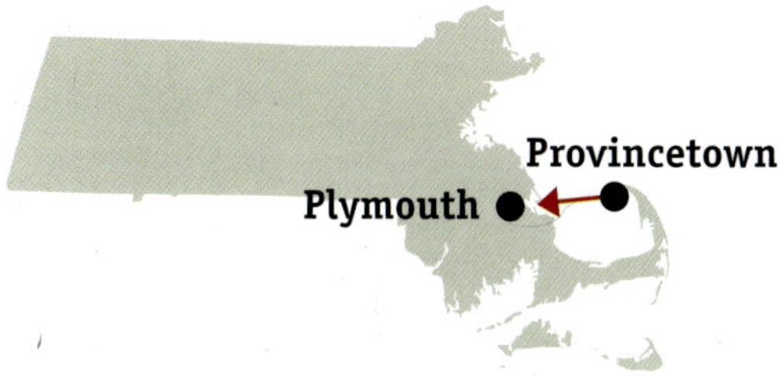

The First Winter

It was now December. The Pilgrims would have to build houses, one at a time. The ground was frozen, so the people stayed on the ship until they could build houses on the shore.

The men made a plan for their town. They built a simple ***meetinghouse.*** There they could worship together and talk about new laws for their colony. They planned to build two rows of houses. They hunted deer in the woods and fished in the ocean to get food for their families.

It was cold and wet on the ship. There were no heaters. As hard as the people worked, they could not keep everyone warm and well fed. About half of the Pilgrims got sick and died that winter.

"Of a hundred persons, **scarce** fifty remain . . . the living are [hardly] able to bury the dead."
—William Bradford

Plimoth or Plymouth?

Why do you see Plimoth spelled different ways? In the 1600s, there were no rules for spelling English words. A writer went by how the word sounded.

When William Bradford wrote his book *Of Plimoth Plantation*, his most common way of spelling it was P-l-i-m-o-t-h. That is why we spell it that way whenever we talk about the village the Pilgrims settled.

Memory Master

Lesson 1

1. Why did the Pilgrims come to America?
2. What was the Mayflower Compact?
3. Where did the Pilgrims first land? Where did they decide to settle?
4. What was life like during the first winter?

Lesson 2

Help From the Wampanoag

PEOPLE TO KNOW
Massasoit
Hobbamock
Samoset
Squanto

PLACES TO LOCATE
Europe
Spain
Maine
Plimoth

WORDS TO UNDERSTAND
defend
explorer
interpreter
point of view
slave
survive
treaty

The Wampanoag Help the Pilgrims

In early spring, a tall man with long black hair walked into Plimoth. He carried a bow and two arrows. He spoke a little English and told the Pilgrims his name was Samoset. He had learned English from fishermen along the coast of Maine. He had once been a great chief there. Samoset told the Pilgrims that a terrible disease had killed most of his people.

When Samoset left Plimoth, he said he would come back with Massasoit, the sachem of the Wampanoag people.

Massasoit's Visit

A short time later, Massasoit and about 20 other Wampanoag men came to Plimoth. The sachem said he wanted to be friends. He hoped the Pilgrims would be on his side against other tribes who were his enemies. He also hoped to trade furs for wool blankets and metal pots and pans.

The Pilgrims gave Massasoit what food and drink they could give. Together they smoked the pipe Massasoit had brought.

Making a Promise

The Pilgrims and the Wampanoag signed a ***treaty.*** A treaty is like a promise that is written down. Here is what the people from each group promised:

- Neither the Pilgrims nor the Wampanoag would harm one another.
- Anyone who harmed either group would be punished.
- The Pilgrims and the Wampanoag would ***defend*** each other in war.
- When visiting each other, they would leave their weapons behind.

For more than 50 years, no one broke the treaty.

Samoset and Squanto Teach the Pilgrims

Massasoit went back to his village. He asked Samoset and another man, Squanto, to help the Pilgrims.

Samoset and Squanto lived along the stream near Plimoth. They helped the Pilgrims learn about the land. They taught them how to plant corn, beans, and squash. They showed them better ways to fish and hunt. They also taught them how to trade with other Indians and sailors in the area.

Soon the Pilgrims were eating well. They were trading with the nearby tribes and European ship captains who sailed near the shore from time to time. Without help from the Wampanoag, the Pilgrims might not have ***survived.***

The Pilgrims must have been happy when spring came. With help from their new friends, they planted wheat, barley, corn, and peas. They kept building homes and planting gardens.

What do you think?

How were the Indians and the Pilgrims alike? How were they different?

Hobbamock was a friend of Massasoit. He brought his family to Plimoth to live with the Pilgrims. This is what his home looked like. Hobbamock helped the Pilgrims as a guide and interpreter. He took groups of men to trade with other tribes.

Massachusetts PORTRAIT

Squanto
1585–1622

Squanto's real name was Tisquantum. He had lived at Plimoth before, when it was an Indian village called Patuxet. An English ship captain had kidnapped him and sold him as a ***slave*** in Spain. Then a Spanish priest helped him escape to England. He sailed back to his home, but his village was empty. Everyone had died of disease brought by European ***explorers*** and fishermen.

Squanto walked until he came to a Wampanoag village. Massasoit became his leader. Massasoit sent Squanto to Plimoth to help the Pilgrims.

Squanto taught the Pilgrims how to plant corn the Indian way. He showed them how to hunt deer, make maple syrup, and catch fish. He also showed them where to trap and trade beaver furs.

Squanto helped as an ***interpreter.*** This means he took the English words of the Pilgrims and said them as Indian words. Then he took the Indian words and said them in English for the Pilgrims. This was a very important job. It helped the two groups understand each other.

Giving Thanks

By the end of the summer, the Pilgrims had many reasons to celebrate. Many fields of corn had grown. Everyone had enough to eat. The fur trade was doing well. Sturdy wooden houses were going up for every family.

The people had celebrated the harvest each year in England. This year they were even more thankful because they had struggled so much and worked so hard.

Governor Bradford said the Pilgrims must thank God for all their blessings. He sent four men out to hunt for food. They brought back enough animals to feed all the Pilgrims for a week.

The Wampanoag were used to thanking the Great Spirit when there was a good harvest. They thanked him every day for his gifts, just as the Pilgrims thanked their God. Some of the Wampanoag came to join in the feast. They went out and hunted too. They brought back five deer for the feast.

The food at the first Thanksgiving was different from the turkey and pie most Americans eat today. The Pilgrims and Indians probably ate ducks, geese, venison (deer), wild turkey, eel, clams, cod, pumpkins, and corn.

Coming Together

There are many ways people give thanks around the world. We call the feast the "first Thanksgiving," but not because it was the first time the Pilgrims or the Indians gave thanks for food. We call it that because it was probably the first time these two cultures came together to offer thanks.

Activity

How Do We Know?

How do we know what happened at the Thanksgiving feast? Two of the Pilgrims who were there wrote about it. Here is what one of them wrote:

> Our harvest being gotten in, our governour sent foure men on fowling, that so we might after a special manner rejoyce together, after we had gathered the fruits of our labour; they foure in one day killed as much fowle, [to last] almost a weeke, at which time . . . many of the Indians coming amongst us, and . . . their great king Massasoyt, with some nintie men, whom for three dayes we entertained and feasted, and they went out and killed five Deere, which we brought to the Plantation and [gave to] our Governour, . . . and others. And although it was not always so plentifull, . . . by the goodness of God, we are so farre from want, that we often wish you partakers of our plentie.
>
> —Edward Winslow

foure = four
fowling = hunting for ducks or geese
labour = work
farre = far

1. The Pilgrims spoke and wrote differently from how we speak and write today. With the help of your teacher, try to put Winslow's words into your own words.
2. What do you think Winslow meant when he said the Pilgrims were "farre from want?"
3. How many Indian men does he say Massasoit brought with him?
4. There were 52 Pilgrims at the feast. Were there more Indians or Pilgrims there?
5. Does he say anything about women and children at the feast?
6. How long did the people feast together?

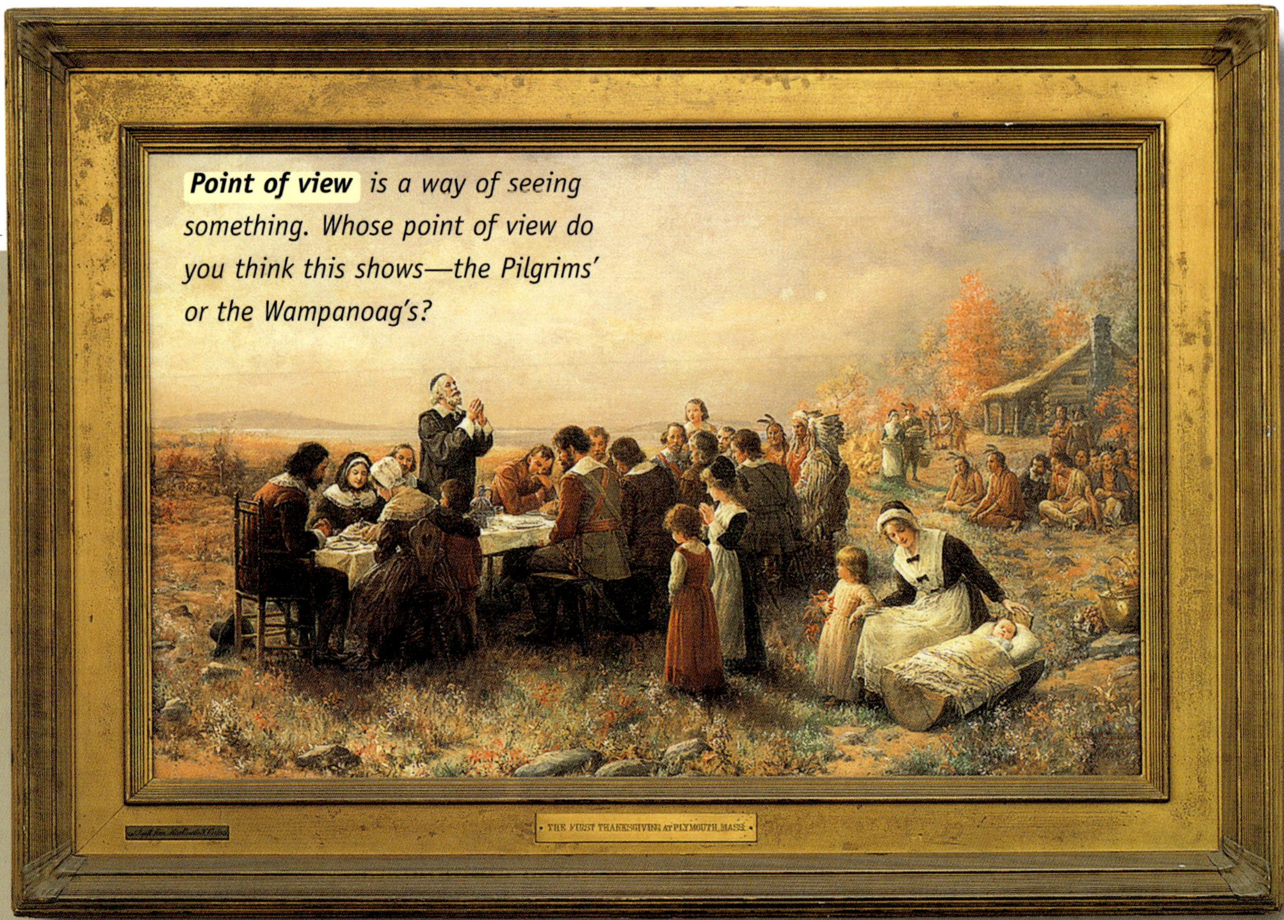

Point of view *is a way of seeing something. Whose point of view do you think this shows—the Pilgrims' or the Wampanoag's?*

Activity

Study a Historic Painting

This painting shows the feast the Pilgrims and Wampanoag shared. There were no photographs back then, so no one knows exactly what the first Thanksgiving feast looked like. An artist made this painting hundreds of years later. He imagined how it might have looked.

1. How many Pilgrims are shown in the picture?
2. How many Wampanoag are shown?
3. Are any women and children shown?
4. Does this match what Edward Winslow wrote?
5. What are the people doing?
6. Do you think a Wampanoag artist would draw the feast in a different way? How might it be different?
7. Do you think the painting shows how the people felt that day?

Memory Master

Lesson 2

1. How did the Wampanoag help the Pilgrims survive? Give two examples.
2. Name two Wampanoag men who helped the Pilgrims.
3. Why was the Thanksgiving feast held?

Everyday Life

The men, women, and children of Plimoth worked hard to make their colony a success.

They lived in tiny one-room houses along the main road of Plimoth. There was a large stone fireplace inside each house. It was used for cooking and heating. The families ate, worked, and spent most of their time near the fireplace. It gave them light and kept them warm.

Each evening, the family read the Bible together. When it was time to sleep, the parents stayed downstairs. The children climbed a ladder to a loft where they slept on piles of hay.

Lesson 3

Life at Plimoth Colony

PEOPLE TO KNOW
Barbara Standish
Myles Standish

PLACES TO LOCATE
Plimoth Colony
Aptucxet
Massachusetts Bay

WORDS TO UNDERSTAND
challenge
cooperation
drought
found
legacy
livestock
musket
opportunity
trading post

Today there is a museum where the Pilgrims' village was. It is a living history museum. That means the people who work there try to look and act just like the Pilgrims did. They speak like the Pilgrims and use only the tools the Pilgrims had. The museum is called Plimoth Plantation. If you visit, you can see what life was really like in the 1620s.

Massachusetts
PORTRAIT

Myles Standish
1584–1656

Myles Standish was on the *Mayflower* when it landed in America. He led the group of men who went ashore to find a good place to settle. As a soldier, he was in charge of making the village safe. He helped the Pilgrims move the cannon they had brought onto a nearby hill.

Myles Standish's wife died that first terrible winter. He married again and had seven children with his new wife, Barbara.

As time passed, the settlers and Native Americans did not stay friends. Standish helped the Pilgrims build a fence around the village. He led fights against the tribes in the area.

As more settlers came on ships across the ocean, they started to build new towns. Standish helped to *found* the town of Duxbury.

You can visit a monument to Myles Standish at Captain's Hill.

The Men of Plimoth

The men spent nearly every day working in the fields near Plimoth. They grew corn, beans, and squash just like the Indians did. They took care of the livestock. ***Livestock*** are animals that are raised for their meat, eggs, or milk. The men also hunted deer and turkeys in the woods.

The Pilgrims began trading with more Indian tribes. Soon they were setting up ***trading posts.*** These were places where people from different areas could meet to trade. The Indians brought beaver furs to the posts. They traded the furs for pots, pans, and other goods.

Aptucxet Trading Post

Aptucxet was the first English trading post in North America. It is still there today.

The Pilgrims set up a trading post at Aptucxet. They wanted to trade with Dutch settlers in New York and the Indians of Cape Cod. They needed a place in the middle where they could meet.

Aptucxet was a good place because each group could travel most of the way by water. It was easier and faster to travel by water than any other way.

Sometimes they traded goods for other goods. Sometimes they traded for wampum. People began to use wampum like we use money today.

After cows were brought from England, the Pilgrims could have milk and beef.

The Women of Plimoth

Women helped the colony feel more like home. Their hard work made a good life possible in the colony. They cooked the food and made all the clothes for the family. They made candles, soap, and anything else the family needed. They kept the house clean. They took care of small gardens near the house. They took care of the children. They also took care of the sick. They made sure a real sense of family and home grew at Plimoth.

The Children of Plimoth

Children had important jobs too. Boys helped their fathers with the crops and livestock. The older boys chopped wood and learned to hunt. They would need these skills when they grew up.

Girls also learned skills for when they grew up. They helped their mothers cook, clean, and sew. They took care of the younger children in the family. They worked in the garden and fed the chickens in the yard.

Both boys and girls had to learn how to read. After a hard day of work, children sat down with their parents by the fire. They learned to read using the Bible. Everyone at Plimoth read the Bible and sang songs from the hymn book at church.

Challenges in a New Land

Have you ever faced a ***challenge?*** A challenge is a kind of test. It is something that stands in your way. It takes hard work to get through it. The Pilgrims faced many challenges in their new home.

The land in America was new to the Pilgrims. They had to learn where the rivers and streams were. They had to learn which plants were harmful and which plants they could use. They had to learn what crops would grow.

Nature was not always kind. There was no bug spray to keep away the insects. Sometimes a fire burned down a house. Often there was no rain for a long time. This is called a ***drought.*** One year a drought ruined the crops. The people had to get all their food by fishing and digging for clams.

The Pilgrims only had the supplies they had brought on the ship. They didn't have cows at first, so there was no milk, cheese, butter, or beef. They did not have enough food to get all the vitamins they needed. If they got sick, there were no doctors' offices or hospitals like there are today. When a disease broke out, many people died.

The Pilgrims missed their loved ones back in England. They were very far from home, and they might never go back. They probably felt lonely, but they did their best to make Plimoth feel like home.

Activity

Write About a Personal Experience

1. It takes courage to face a challenge. Courage is being brave. If you have courage, you are willing to try something new.
   - Can you think of how the Pilgrims showed courage?
   - Can you think of how the Wampanoag showed courage?
2. The Pilgrims worked together. This is called ***cooperation.*** They helped each other build homes. They helped each other hunt and find food. They knew they could not survive if they did not work together. The Indians and the Pilgrims also cooperated. By working together, they learned from each other.
3. Think of a time when you have shown courage or cooperation. Write a short essay about it. Start each sentence with a capital letter. Use complete sentences to explain how you showed courage or cooperation.

The Legacy of the Pilgrims

Over the next few years, ships brought supplies from England. Ships also brought more people. Some hoped to practice their own faith. Others wanted to farm or set up a trade. They believed they could have a better life in Massachusetts.

Explorers and fishermen had come to Massachusetts, but until the Pilgrims came, none had been able to start a colony here. The Pilgrims believed in self-government. They honored the law. They worked hard and lived what they believed. They showed the world that America could be a place of freedom and ***opportunity.***

Plimoth Colony never grew very large. Soon there was a larger colony at Massachusetts Bay. But Plimoth's ***legacy,*** or gift to the future, lives on.

This spoon belonged to a family of Pilgrims. They had to think of all the little things they might need in their new home. Would you have thought to bring a spoon? What else would you have brought with you?

"Build your cabins as open as you can, and bring good store of clothes and bedding with you . . . bring every man a ***musket*** . . . bring juice of lemons . . . if you bring any thing for comfort, let it be butter or salted oil . . . bring paper and linseed oil for your windows with cotton yarn for your lamps . . . bring store of powder and shot."

—Edward Winslow

Lesson 3

Memory Master

1. List two jobs the men of Plimoth did.
2. List two jobs the women did.
3. List two jobs the children did.
4. What challenges did the Pilgrims face in their new home?

Chapter 4 Review

What's the Point?

The Pilgrims were not free to practice their religion in England. They sailed to Massachusetts on the *Mayflower*. They made a set of laws for themselves, called the Mayflower Compact.

The Pilgrims settled at Plimoth. They had a hard time at first. The Wampanoag people who lived nearby helped them survive. They taught the Pilgrims how to fish, hunt, and plant crops. At harvest time, the Pilgrims and the Wampanoag shared a feast of thanksgiving.

The Pilgrims built a village they called Plimoth Plantation. It grew as more people and supplies came from England.

Activity

Cause and Effect

Sometimes when we do something, it causes something else to happen. When we enter a dark room and flip on the light switch, the room is filled with light. This is called cause and effect. The cause is flipping on the light switch. The effect is that the room is filled with light.

Life is filled with causes and effects. So is history. The things people did caused other things to happen.

CAUSE: Action that happens first and causes something else to happen

EFFECT: What happened because of the cause

On a piece of paper, write "C" for the cause and "E" for the effect. The first one is done for you.

1. C You start your own church in England in the 1600s.
   E You are put in jail.

2. ____ You get scurvy on the trip across the ocean.
   ____ There is no fresh fruit on board.

3. ____ You run out of supplies.
   ____ You go hungry.

4. ____ The Pilgrims had enough food to eat.
   ____ The Wampanoag taught the Pilgrims how to grow crops.

5. ____ You trade something you have.
   ____ You get some of the goods you want.

"The whole life . . . should be praises and thanks to God; we should neither eat nor sleep, but eat to God and sleep to God and work to God and talk to God, do all to His glory and praise."

—Richard Sibbes, a Puritan

The Puritans

Chapter 5

Ten years after the Pilgrims arrived on the Mayflower, *the Puritans came to Massachusetts.*

Lesson 1

Massachusetts Bay Colony

PEOPLE TO KNOW
William Blackstone
Anne Hutchinson
William Pynchon
John Winthrop

PLACES TO LOCATE
England
Connecticut River Valley
Boston
Charlestown
Dorchester
Lynn
Medford
Roxbury
Salem
Springfield
Watertown
Massachusetts Bay

WORDS TO UNDERSTAND
banish
brand
journal
pillory

Who Were the Puritans?

You have learned about the Pilgrims' colony at Plymouth. Another colony was founded in Massachusetts. The Puritans, another group from England, started it.

In England, the Puritans wanted to change the king's church. They said worship should be simple. The king grew angry at the Puritans. He had some of them locked in jail and hanged.

In America, the Puritans could worship God in their own way. They could also be an example of good living for the rest of the world.

A Journey Across the Ocean

John Winthrop led 16 ships across the ocean. There were about 1,000 Puritans on the ships. Winthrop sailed on a ship called the *Arbella*.

Winthrop had heard about the trouble of the Pilgrims in America. He tried to make sure his people had everything they would need. He brought plenty of food, goods to trade, and even cattle.

What Should I Bring?

One man made a list of tools that every family coming to New England would need. Here are some of the things on his list:

scoop	5 broad howes [hoes]	wheels for a cart
great pail	5 narrow howes [hoes]	wheel barrow
casting shovel	5 felling axes	canoe
a sack	2 hand saws	short oak ladder
tobacco pipes	2 hammers	plough [plow]. . .

—John Josselyn, *Two Voyages to New England*

1. Why do you think axes and saws were important?
2. Why do you think a canoe was important?
3. What do you think people might do with a "scoop"?

The Arbella *leads other ships into Massachusetts Bay.*

John Winthrop

A City on a Hill

John Winthrop knew the journey of the Puritans was an important one in history. He gathered the people together on the deck of the *Arbella* and gave a speech. He said:

> *We must consider that we shall be as a city upon a hill. The eyes of all people are upon us.*

After many days at sea, the ships landed in what is now Salem. The people were happy to finally walk on land again.

What do you think?

- Read John Winthrop's words again. What do you think he meant? Try putting his words into your own words.
- How would you feel if you were one of the people listening to Winthrop?

Massachusetts PORTRAIT

John Winthrop
1588–1649

In England, John Winthrop was a lawyer. He owned land and had servants. He lost his job because he was a Puritan. The king did not like Puritans.

Winthrop wanted to live in a place where the people lived by the rules of the Bible. He led a large group of Puritans to Massachusetts.

Winthrop was the first governor of the Massachusetts Bay Colony. He helped the people build a town in the wilderness. He tried to make the colony an example for the world. The colonists chose Winthrop to be their leader 12 times.

John Winthrop was married three times. He and Mary, his first wife, had six children. Mary died, and his second wife died soon after they were married. His third wife, Margaret, waited in England while he set up the colony. Then she joined him in Massachusetts. While they were apart, they said they would think of each other every Monday and Friday between 5:00 and 6:00 p.m.

Winthrop kept a *journal.* A journal is another word for a diary. He wrote about what happened in the colony. We know a lot about the Puritans because of his journal.

Different From the Pilgrims

Both the Puritans and the Pilgrims came across the ocean to settle in Massachusetts. They both came for religious freedom, but the two groups were different. How were the Puritans different from the Pilgrims? Look at the chart to find out.

Pilgrims	Puritans
Came in 1620	Came in 1630
Came on the "Mayflower"	Came on the "Arbella" and other ships
Were led by William Bradford	Were led by John Winthrop
Were a small group	Were a larger group, better prepared for the trip. The people were better educated and had more money.
Wanted to start their own church	Wanted to fix the king's church
Settled at Plymouth	Settled at Salem
Started Plymouth Colony	Started Massachusetts Bay Colony

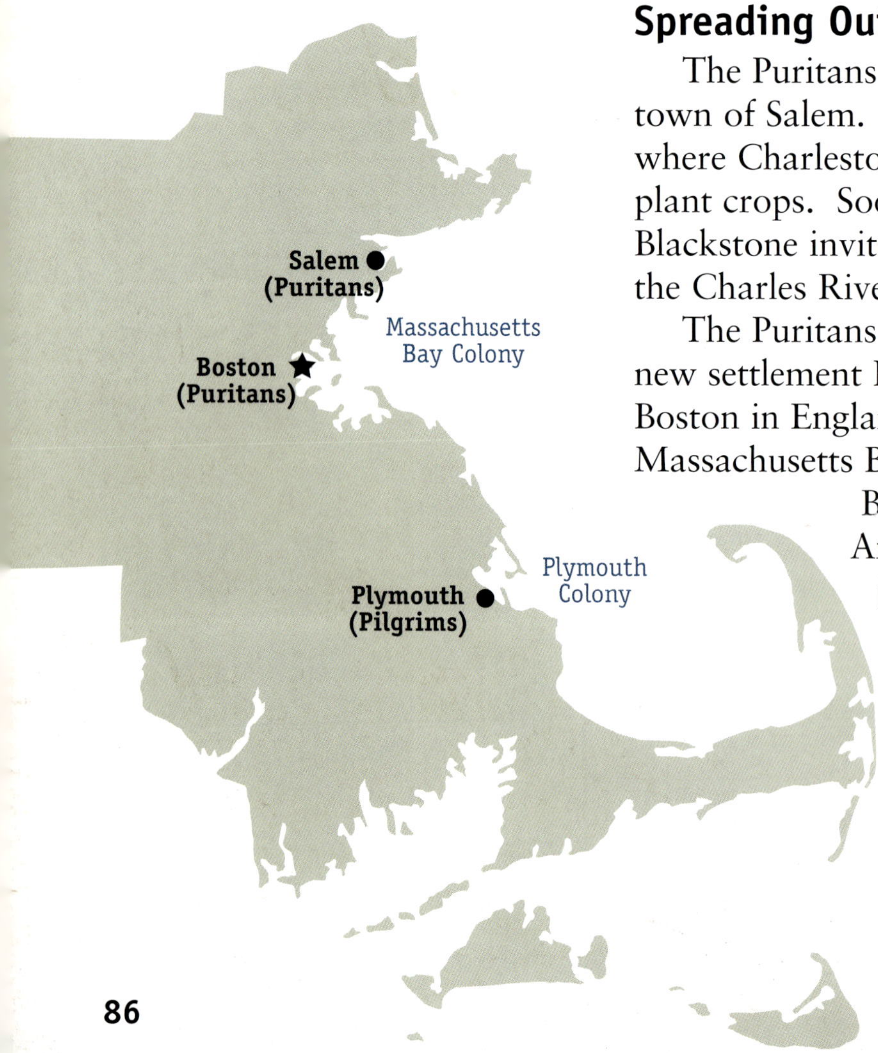

Spreading Out

The Puritans settled along Massachusetts Bay. They built the town of Salem. Not long after, Winthrop took a small group to where Charlestown is now. When they got there, it was too late to plant crops. Soon they were out of food. A man named William Blackstone invited them to come and live near him. He lived across the Charles River.

The Puritans liked it there and decided to stay. They named their new settlement Boston. Many of them had come from a town called Boston in England. The town became the capital of the Massachusetts Bay Colony.

Before long, thousands of Puritans were coming to America. They risked their lives to get here. They joined the others in Salem and Boston. Some started new towns at Lynn, Dorchester, Medford, Watertown, and Roxbury.

What do you think?

- Why do you think the people gave Boston the same name as their town back home?
- If you started a new town, what would you name it?

This picture of Boston in the 1660s shows a tavern and sailing ships in the harbor.

A Puritan Town

Towns were important to the Massachusetts Bay Colony. Puritan families did not go off on their own to start farms. They started towns so they could live and work together. This picture shows some of the things the towns had. What are the people doing? What other buildings do you see?

Farm strips:
The land around the town was divided into strips. Large families were given more strips than small families. Every family was given some good land and some poor land.
House lots and garden plots:
Every family got a plot of land around the town green. They built a house facing the village green. They could grow vegetables and herbs in a garden plot nearby.

The Rule of Law

John Winthrop wanted to make a new and better world for the Puritans. He wanted them to have laws and rules. He wanted their laws to be based on the Bible.

The General Court

A group of leaders from each town made up the General Court. The General Court made the laws for the whole colony.

The people liked being able to choose their own leaders. They liked sending those leaders to speak for them at the General Court. They liked having a say in their own government.

Town Meetings

Once a year the people went to a town meeting. Town meetings were very important. The people got to talk about problems in their town. The men voted on new laws. They chose who would lead their town.

YOUR TOWN

- Many towns in New England still have town meetings. Does your town have them? Ask an adult to tell you what goes on there.
- When was your town founded? See if you can find out from your historical society or on the Internet. What can you learn about your town's religious history?

What do you think?

- Would you like to live in a country with no laws? Why or why not?
- If you lived in colonial times, would you want a king to make the laws for you, or would you want the people in your colony to make their own laws?

The New Colony Grows

More and more Puritans arrived from England. Many stayed in Boston, but others moved on to start new towns.

William Pynchon led settlers west to the Connecticut River Valley. They founded the town of Springfield. The rich soil was excellent for farming. The woods were full of wild animals. Their furs could be traded in Europe for gold. The fish in the river could be caught, dried, and sold to settlers in other colonies.

Governor Winthrop saw that trade could be important. He built a ship called the *Blessing of the Bay*. He began trading furs, dried fish, food, and lumber up and down the Atlantic Coast. Soon every town with a good harbor was building ships. Ships from Massachusetts sailed the waters of the Caribbean Sea, the Atlantic Ocean, and the Mediterranean Sea.

Freedom for All?

Some of the Puritan laws were very strict. The people were cruel to anyone who did not follow their faith or their strict laws. The Puritans came here for religious freedom, but they did not let others have the same freedom.

People who broke the law or disagreed with them about religion were punished. They were hanged, whipped, or ***branded*** with a hot iron. Some were placed in the ***pillory,*** or stocks, on the village green. A person's head, hands, or feet were locked into the wooden stocks. Other people could pass by and look at the criminals.

An English visitor wrote about some of the punishments:

- *For being drunk, they either whip or . . . fine.*
- *For kissing a woman in the street, they either whip or . . . fine.*
- *For swearing or cursing, they bore through the tongue with a hot iron.*
- *For a gossiping woman, they gag her and tie her to a chair in front of her house for everyone to laugh at.*

Memory Master

Lesson 1

1. Who was John Winthrop?
2. List two ways the Puritans were different from the Pilgrims.
3. Where did the Puritans settle?
4. Name one feature of a Puritan town.
5. Why did the people have town meetings?
6. How did the Puritans treat people who had other ideas about religion?

Massachusetts PORTRAIT

Anne Hutchinson
1591–1643

Anne Hutchinson was the mother of 14 children. She loved to listen to sermons in the Puritan Church. She began to hold meetings in her own home where men and women could talk about religion.

Soon Anne Hutchinson was preaching her own ideas about religion. She said God could talk to everyone, and everyone could talk to God. No one needed the Puritan Church or its many ministers.

Governor Winthrop did not like this. He brought Anne Hutchinson to trial. He said she was trying to destroy the rule of law in the colony. But Anne Hutchinson said,

> *What have I said or done except that no man shall think for me?*

Anne was ***banished,*** or sent away, from Massachusetts Bay, along with her husband and children. They moved to Rhode Island and later to New York. In New York, Native Americans killed the entire family except for one child.

Lesson 2

Life in a Puritan Town

PEOPLE TO KNOW
Anne Bradstreet
John Hull

PLACES TO LOCATE
Boston
Cambridge
Ipswich
North Andover
Salem

WORDS TO UNDERSTAND
apprentice
blacksmith
flax
gristmill
hornbook
loom
merchant
militia
muster
pewter
public school

Everyday Life

What was life like for the Puritans? Let's read about the things they did from day to day.

Men, women, and children had special jobs to do. All men between 16 and 60 had to join the ***militia.*** This was a company of soldiers who protected the town. One day a year, the men practiced shooting on the village green. This was called a ***muster.***

Cooking was one of the most important jobs for women. When one meal was over, a mother and her daughters cleaned up and started work on the next meal. Let's see what you would have eaten in colonial days:

Breakfast: Everyone was up just after sunrise. The whole family listened as the father read from the Bible. Then they sat down to steaming porridge served in wooden bowls. Porridge was made by boiling milk and flour or cornmeal together.

Dinner: This was the big meal of the day. It was served at noon when the men and boys came in from the fields. Women usually made a stew called succotash. Today we think of succotash as beans and corn. In the days of the Puritans, it was made of meat, peas, corn, and other vegetables. Everyone got a heaping serving of succotash in a ***pewter*** dish. Pewter is a type of tin used to make spoons, forks, cups, bowls, and pitchers.

Supper: Supper came after sundown when the day's work was done. The adults ate cold meat and bread. They drank beer or apple cider. The children ate "hasty pudding" made from cornmeal and milk. No one drank milk in those days. People did not think it was healthy.

Puritans used pewter dishes like this one at home and at church.

Courtesy of PVMA, Memorial Hall Museum, Deerfield, MA

▶ Photo ©Kindra Clineff

What is the biggest thing in this room? The fireplace! Why was it so big? The women cooked over the fire. They had to be able to take pots in and out and roast meat over the coals. The fireplace was also the heater for the whole house. In the evening, the fire gave light for reading or sewing.

What kinds of things do you see on top of the fireplace?

This woman has spun wool into yarn. She will use the yarn to make clothes for the family. What do you see in the baskets at her feet?

Courtesy of Historic Deerfield

These modern girls are dressed up like Puritans.

*This is a spinning wheel. Women and girls used it to turn **flax** into thread. They also spun wool from their sheep into yarn. Next they used a **loom** to weave the thread into cloth.*

Courtesy of PVMA Memorial Hall Museum, Deerfield, MA

A Young Girl's Work

Pretend you are a young Puritan girl. You help your mother cook and serve the food. You wash the dishes and clean the house from top to bottom. You help take care of the younger children. You help in the garden.

You also help make the family's clothes. You spin thread and weave cloth. You learn how to knit. You practice by the fire at night.

When the clothes are dirty, you take them outside and wash them by hand. You even make the soap. You learn these things so you can take care of your own home and family one day.

A Young Boy's Work

Pretend you are a young Puritan boy. It is your job to chop wood and bring it in for the fire. You feed the chickens and horses. You clean the barn. In the garden, you pick berries, pull weeds, and gather vegetables. Sometimes you run errands for your parents.

By the time you are 10 or 12, you have to think about what you will do for a living. You can do what your father does, or you can learn a new trade. Maybe you will decide to go to college and become a minister or a lawyer.

Time to Play

The children still had time to play. They made their own toys. They made dolls from cornhusks or apples. They carved a face on an apple and let it dry. The children played games such as tag, marbles, leapfrog, and hopscotch. They played nine pins, which is like bowling. They had sack races and rolled a large hoop with a stick.

In winter, the family often climbed in the wagon and set out across the fields on a sleigh ride. It was fun to bundle up in blankets. The bells jingled as the horses trotted along. Back home by the fire, children played with dolls and made paper hats.

At special times, adults and children lined up and danced. They listened to music from violins, guitars, English flutes, and harpsichords (kind of like small pianos). They also used their voices to make music.

Early colonists put hot coals in this metal box. They used it as a foot warmer. On cold days, they brought it to church or put it in their wagon.

Going to Meeting

On Sundays, a ringing bell told the people it was time for church. They went to services in the morning. They went home or to the tavern for a cold lunch. Cooking was not allowed on Sunday. After lunch they went back to church. It was hard for children to sit still for so long, but they did their best.

There were no heaters in the meetinghouse. Sometimes the minister preached with his coat and mittens on. People brought heated stones or coals to help them keep warm.

Photo by Joan Grossman, Courtesy of the Amherst History Museum

Puritan Schools

Learning was very important. In the early years of the colony, parents taught their children how to read and write. They used the Bible as a textbook.

Soon, people wanted schools. Boston set up the Latin School. It was the first ***public school.*** (That means the people of Boston paid for it, not just the parents of the boys who went there.) Young boys could go to the school and learn Latin and Greek for free. They needed to know these languages if they wanted to go to college.

There were laws about going to school. Every town had to teach boys who had no parents to teach them. When a town had 50 families, it had to have an elementary school. There children learned to read, write, and do simple math. Every town with 100 families had to have a Latin grammar school. It would get young boys ready for college.

During this time, girls could not go to the schools. Some girls went to "dame schools" to learn how to read and write. Older women set up these schools in their own homes.

If you were lucky enough to go to school, you learned from a ***hornbook.*** *A hornbook was a wooden paddle with a sheet of paper attached to it. The alphabet and words from the Bible were printed on the paper. A clear piece of animal horn was placed over the paper to protect it. You may have also used* The New England Primer. *It was the first textbook.*

Harvard is in Cambridge, Massachusetts.

Because of the laws and Puritan rules about reading the Bible, many people in the Massachusetts Bay Colony could read and write. In the other colonies, fewer people knew how.

Harvard College

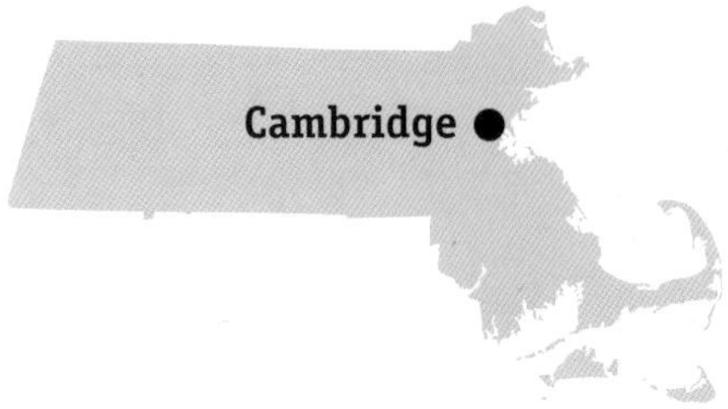

The people of Massachusetts decided they needed a college. The Puritans started Harvard College in Cambridge in 1636. It was the first college in America.

The college was named for John Harvard. He was a young man who had recently died and left some money and his library to the new college.

How did a boy know when he was ready to go to Harvard College? Here is the rule he was to follow:

> *When any scholar is able to understand Latin authors, and make and speak true Latin . . . and [say] the nouns and verbs in . . . Greek . . ., let him then . . . be capable of admission to the college.*

Massachusetts PORTRAIT

Anne Bradstreet
1612–1672

One busy mother had time to become America's first great poet. Her name was Anne Bradstreet. She was only 18 when she sailed with her husband on the *Arbella* to the Massachusetts Bay Colony.

In England, she had been a wealthy girl with many servants. Now she was in a wilderness where she had to work hard just to survive. She decided to think of this new life as a gift from God.

The Bradstreets moved many times, each time farther into the western wilderness. They started out in Cambridge, then moved to Ipswich, and later to North Andover.

During these years, Anne began writing poetry. She often wrote at night when her children had gone to bed. She wrote her poems only for her family. She was surprised when her brother-in-law had them published in England.

Her best poems told of her deep love for her family. She wrote these words in a poem about her husband:

If ever two were one, then surely we,
If ever man were loved by wife, then thee,
If ever wife was happy in a man,
Compare with me ye women if you can.

Making a Living

Farmers

Most people were farmers. They had fields at the edge of town. The father and older sons left the house at dawn to work on the farm. They worked all day long during the wet spring and hot summer. They chopped down trees, planted crops, and took care of the animals.

The mother and older daughters stayed at the house in town. They cooked, cleaned, and sewed for the family. They took care of the garden. The young children helped in the fields and around the house. They took the cows to pasture every morning and brought them back to the barn at night.

Merchants

More people were starting to trade for a living. They saved their money, bought a few ships, and began sailing the waters of the Atlantic. They soon made fortunes by carrying goods between the colonies and Europe, Africa, and the West Indies. These people were called ***merchants.***

Some merchants became rich. They built large homes in Boston and Salem. They filled their homes with fine furniture. Their wives wore the latest fashions from Europe. Their children went to the best schools in England. Many colonists looked up to the merchants as the leaders of Massachusetts.

The Rise of John Hull

John Hull was born in England. When John was still a boy, he came to Massachusetts with the rest of his family. He worked long hours on the family farm and in his father's blacksmith shop. By the time he was 18, he wanted to move to Boston. There he hoped to make more money.

John Hull became a merchant. Not everyone became as wealthy as he did, but most believed that if they worked hard and stuck to their goals, they could have a better life.

This was not possible in England. In England, a better life was possible for the king's family or the lords and ladies, but not for the common people.

Most towns had a miller. He ran the ***gristmill,*** *where grain was ground into flour. The miller used the power of a river to turn the millstone. The moving stone ground the grain.*

Carpenter

Craftsmen

Some people made money by making things to sell to others. They might make shoes, barrels, or candles. A ***blacksmith*** knew how to make iron into tools. He made horseshoes, nails, ladles, axe heads, and other things people used every day.

Craftsmen always needed helpers. Some young men worked for them as ***apprentices.*** An apprentice lived with the craftsman and learned his skills. The craftsman gave the apprentice food, clothes, and a place to live, but he did not pay him money.

Blacksmith

Memory Master

Lesson 2

1. List two ways of making a living in the Massachusetts Bay Colony.
2. List two jobs that women did.
3. Puritan children learned to read and write so they could read the ____________.

Lesson 3

Changes in the Colony

PEOPLE TO KNOW
King Philip (Metacom)
Massasoit
Betty Parris
Tituba

PLACES TO LOCATE
Maine
Deerfield
Petersham
Salem

WORDS TO UNDERSTAND
accuse
content
flattering

"My father gave them what they asked . . . they have towns and whole kingdoms for a few blankets, hoes, and ***flattering*** words . . . and still they are not ***content!***"

—King Philip (Metacom)

War With Native Americans

The Massachusetts Bay Colony was a great success. Towns were spreading out to the Connecticut River Valley. Merchants took goods from Massachusetts all around the Atlantic Ocean. To many people, the future seemed bright.

But the future was not bright for the Native people. They watched as the colonists cut down more trees to make homes. The colonists cleared more fields to plant crops. They scared away many animals. It was hard for the tribes to find good land to grow crops. It was hard to find enough animals to feed their families in the winter. They decided they had to fight for their land.

Do you remember reading about Massasoit, the great sachem of the Wampanoag people? King Philip was his son. His real name was Metacom, but the colonists called him "King Philip." He brought all the tribes in the area together to fight colonists throughout New England.

King Philip's War went on for more than a year. Both sides fought hard and lost many lives, but the Indians lost more. The colonists killed King Philip and posted his head on a stake at Plymouth for the next 25 years.

At first, the colonists probably would not have survived in America without help from Native Americans. But before long, the colonists treated Native Americans as if they were just in the way.

England Takes Control

Just as the colony was getting back on its feet, England decided to make big changes.

England wanted more control over its colonies. In 1691, it made Plymouth Colony and the Massachusetts Bay Colony into one colony. Maine was also part of Massachusetts during this time. The King of England made new laws about trading. He also wanted to choose the new governors.

The colonists were used to making their own laws. They did not like the king taking over like this.

The Salem Witch Trials 1692

The changes in the colony scared many people. They wondered if they had failed to become the "city on a hill." Was it their fault, or was something evil at work in the colony? Perhaps, some thought, the devil himself was loose in Massachusetts.

Young Girls Fall Ill

Betty Parris was a young Salem girl. During the winter, her friends often came over to pass the time. They listened to stories from Tituba, the Parris' slave. Tituba told them about witches and spells.

Betty Parris began to act in a strange way. She had fits, where she danced around and cried out. Soon Abigail Williams, Ann Putnam, and other girls in town were acting the same way. The doctor could not say why. He said maybe it was witchcraft.

The people of Salem were certain that witches were everywhere. A witch was someone who helped the devil do his evil in the world.

The girls were asked who was making them act this way. They said Tituba was. Tituba and the girls said there were secret witches among the Puritans.

Fear Spreads Through the Town

Everyone was afraid. They started *accusing* others of being witches. They looked at their friends and neighbors and thought, "Is she a witch?" "Is he a witch?"

More girls had fits of fainting and shaking. They said the witches sent ghosts to harm them. Before long, hundreds of people were put in jail. A special court was set up to hear the cases. There was very little proof, but many people were found guilty of being witches.

> *I am innocent. I know nothing of it. I have done no witchcraft.*
>
> *—Bridget Bishop*

Punishment for "Witches"

If you were found to be a witch, there was not much you could do. The punishment was hanging. Nineteen people were hanged. Giles Corey said he would not go to trial, so he was pressed to death with heavy stones. Others sat in the damp dark jail for months.

An End to the Trials

Finally, the governor had seen enough. He ended the Salem witch trials. In time, the people told the families they were sorry.

This is a statue of Roger Conant, the founder of Salem. It stands next to the Salem Witch Museum, but Roger Conant was not part of the witch trials. He died before they started. What do you think he might have thought about what happened in his town?

Growing Cities and Towns

As the 1700s began, the colony grew. Cities such as Boston had more and more buildings. More people started new towns. Older towns split to form new towns. Over time, Dedham became six towns.

Settlers moved farther west, where the land was better for farming. They founded towns such as Belchertown, Deerfield, and Stockbridge.

New Roads

The first roads followed old Indian trails. The people wanted better roads to link new towns to Boston and other cities. Workers cleared away the trees and built new roads.

Along the roads, people built taverns and inns. Travelers stopped there to eat and rest. The sign at Nash's Tavern in Amherst said, "Drink for the thirsty, Food for the hungry, Lodging for the weary, and Good keeping for the horses."

Taverns were also for the people who lived in the towns. They had meetings, dances, and elections there. People went to the tavern to eat, relax, meet friends, gossip, and talk about the news.

Clearing More Land

Timber was easy to get in New England. There were forests full of trees. Shipbuilders needed wood to build ships. Loggers cut down trees and sent them to sawmills to be cut. Timber was also sold to other colonies.

Farmers cut down trees too. They cleared the land for crops and pastures. They moved heavy rocks out of the way and stacked them into walls to mark their fields. Before long, there were open spots of land here and there. Look at the pictures to see how Petersham changed over time.

Jobs in Colonial Massachusetts

In the growing cities and towns, there were many jobs to do. These were some of the jobs in colonial Massachusetts.

Barber/Wig Maker

Butcher

Cabinet Maker

In 1700, people found the land covered with trees.

Here is the same land after farmers and loggers began clearing it.

By the end of the 1700s, most of the trees were gone.

Attack at Deerfield

The land in the Connecticut River Valley was home to the Pocumtuck and many other Indian peoples. They had lived there for many thousands of years.

By the late 1600s, English colonists were moving into the Connecticut River Valley. Some of them settled in the homeland of the Indians already living there. These colonists built a small farming village near the river and called it Deerfield.

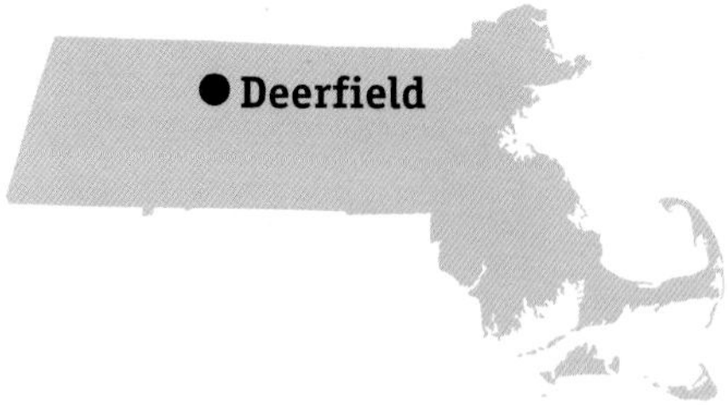

Like England, France also claimed land in North America. France and England were often at war at this time. Both the French and Native people wanted to drive the English out of western Massachusetts and Maine. French soldiers and Native warriors often joined together to raid English settlements that were in Indian homelands.

This meant that colonists in places like Deerfield lived in fear. Many times Native warriors and French soldiers attacked their settlements. They burned houses and killed or captured people. They also ruined or took crops. Deerfield and other towns built fences and asked the governor to send soldiers to help protect them. Sometimes the colonists left these towns and moved somewhere else.

The biggest attack came at Deerfield in February, 1704. About 250 French soldiers and members of several different Indian groups attacked just before dawn. More than 40 English soldiers and settlers were killed. Over 100 more were taken captive. The captive men, women and children had to walk through the snow all the way to Canada. Over time, some of the captives came back to Deerfield. Others chose to stay and live with the French and Indians.

Many Voices

There are many stories about what happened at Deerfield. Each group that was there has a different story to tell. To understand the past, we must listen to many voices. Today, places like the Memorial Hall Museum in Deerfield let us do just that. They show us many points of view. To learn about the "Many Stories of 1704," visit their website:

www.1704.deerfield.history.museum

Memory Master

Lesson 3

1. Why did King Philip lead Native Americans in a war against the colonists?
2. What were the Salem witch trials?
3. What kinds of things did people do at a colonial tavern?
4. Give one example of how things changed as the cities and towns in the colony grew.

Patrick Tracy by Jonathan Trumbull, 1784/1786

Study a Historic Painting

Some wealthy people had their portraits painted. They hung them in the grand rooms of their homes. This is a portrait of Patrick Tracy. He was from Newburyport. Answer the questions to see if you can learn more about Patrick Tracy.

1. Look at his clothes. What kind of people wore these clothes? Look at some of the other pictures of people in this chapter. How are their clothes the same or different from Patrick Tracy's?
2. Where is he standing? What is behind him? What do you see on the left side of the picture?
3. What is his hand resting on?
4. Look at his face. About how old do you think he was when this painting was made? Does the look on his face tell you anything about his character?
5. From all of these clues, can you guess what Patrick Tracy did for a living? Would you guess a farmer, a fisherman, a miller, a craftsman, or a merchant?

Chapter 5 Review

What's the Point?

The Puritans were not free to worship in England. They came across the ocean and started the Massachusetts Bay Colony. They settled first in Salem and Boston. As more people came, they built new towns.

As more colonists settled on the land, more Native Americans lost their land. They fought the colonists in King Philip's War, but they were defeated.

The king of England made Plymouth Colony and the Massachusetts Bay Colony into one colony. The people of colonial Massachusetts worked hard to take care of their families and to make a better life.

Activity

Pilgrims or Puritans?

Now that you have learned about both the Pilgrims and the Puritans, can you remember which is which? Read each sentence below. Write PG if it is about the Pilgrims of Plymouth. Write PR if it is about the Puritans of Massachusetts Bay.

1. ________ They came in 1630.
2. ________ They came on the *Mayflower*.
3. ________ They said they would be like a "city on a hill."
4. ________ They cooperated with the Native Americans.
5. ________ They came in 1620.
6. ________ They did not bring cattle with them.
7. ________ They came on 16 ships.
8. ________ Many died during the first year.
9. ________ They killed many people accused of being witches.
10. ________ They fought with the Native Americans.

Massachusetts in the American Revolution

'One if by land, and two if by sea;
And I on the opposite shore will be,
Ready to ride and spread the alarm
Through every Middlesex village and farm,
For the country folk to be up and to arm.'

—from "Paul Revere's Ride"
by Henry Wadsworth Longfellow

Chapter 6

The first battles of the American Revolution were fought in Massachusetts towns. Farmers and craftsmen in Lexington and Concord grabbed their guns and went to fight for liberty.

Lesson 1

Trouble Brews

PEOPLE TO KNOW
Sam Adams
Crispus Attucks
Paul Revere

PLACES TO LOCATE
England
Boston
Concord

WORDS TO UNDERSTAND
bayonet
congress
independence
Loyalist
massacre
minuteman
Patriot
protest
representative
revolution
tax
wharf

English people are also called British.

Trouble With England

The story of the American Revolution is the story of how our country came to be. A ***revolution*** is when people fight to replace one government with a different government.

Taxes and More Taxes

By the 1760s, England had 13 colonies in America. Massachusetts was one of the colonies.

The British needed money to pay for wars they had fought. They needed to pay for soldiers sent to America to protect the colonists from the Indians. To raise money, they taxed the colonists. A ***tax*** is money people must pay to the government.

The British taxed things such as sugar and molasses. The colonists used these things almost every day. They put sugar in their tea. They used molasses for baking. Soon there were taxes on glass, paper, paint, and tea. The colonists drank tea every day. A tax on tea would cost a lot of money.

Then came the Stamp Act. It said that certain papers the colonists used had to have special stamps on them. The colonists had to pay for the stamps. Letters, newspapers, and even playing cards had to have the stamps.

"No Taxation Without Representation"

The colonists did not have a say in what laws or taxes were passed in England. They wanted to send a few people to England to speak for them. But England would not let the colonists send ***representatives*** to government meetings.

Many colonists thought this was unfair. They did not think England should make rules for them without letting them vote. They said, "No taxation without representation!"

The Colonists Protest

The colonists were very unhappy about the taxes. They would not pay the stamp tax. They wrote letters saying it was unfair.

They found other ways to *protest.* One way was to stop buying British goods. The people stopped buying tea, sugar, cloth, and other items from British merchants.

To get things back in control, the British sent soldiers to Boston. Most of the soldiers stayed in the homes of the colonists. The colonists did not like having the soldiers so close.

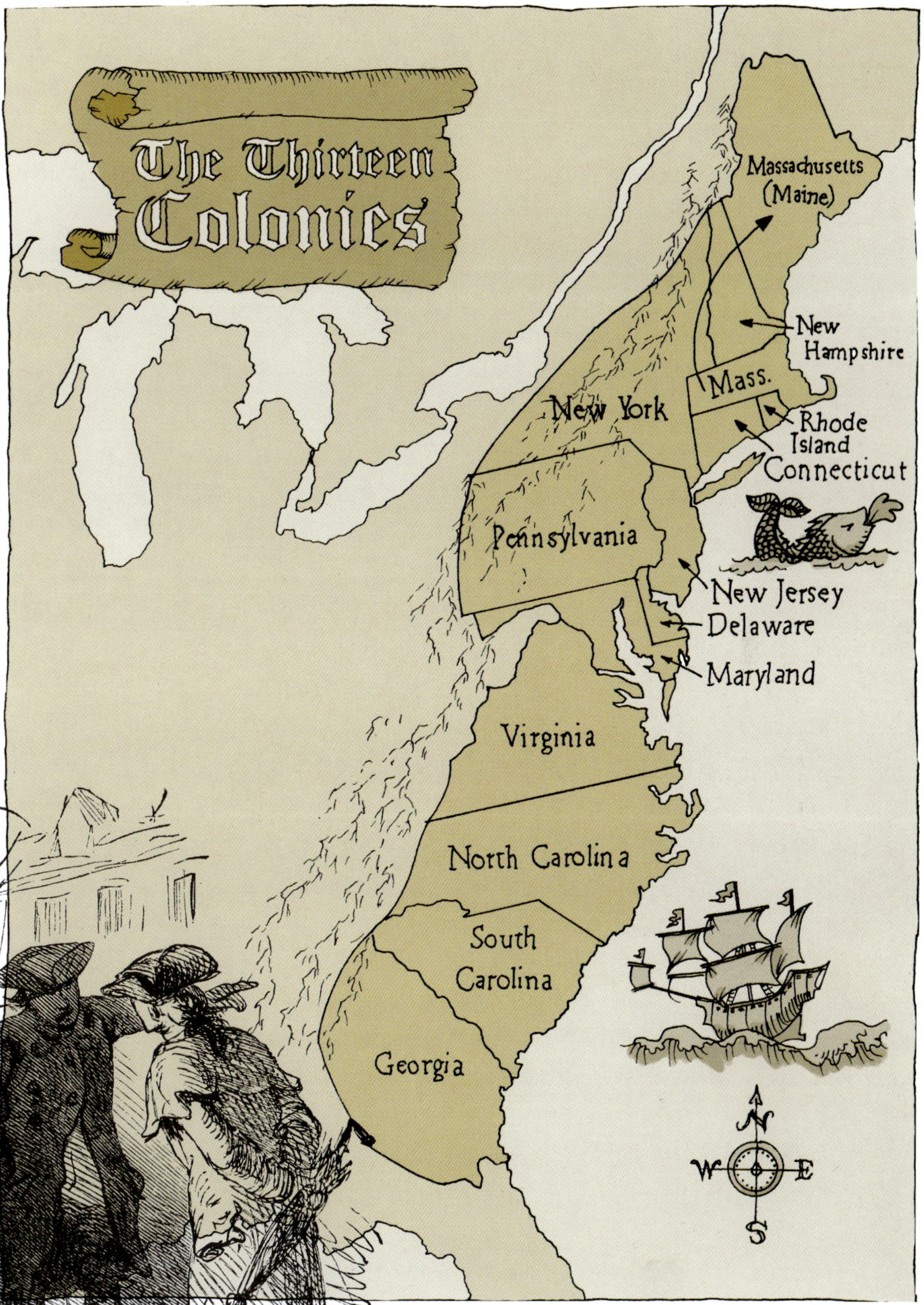

The colonists argued with the British over the taxes.

The Boston Massacre

If You Were There

It is cold and dark on the night of March 5, 1770. You are sitting with friends in the tavern when you hear some noise outside. You rub the frosty window and look out into the street. You see a mob of men and boys arguing with a British guard.

You have heard your father and the other men talk about the British soldiers. No one wants them in Boston. You've heard people in the town calling the soldiers names.

You slip out the door and into the snow to see what is going on. People are shouting. They gather in front of the Customs House, where the taxes are paid.

You hear angry words shouted back and forth. You shiver when you see the guard push a young man with his sharp ***bayonet.*** The next thing you know, the church bell is ringing in alarm. At this sound, more people join you in the street.

The men tease the guard. You are too scared and cold to shout with them, but you hear them call his name and dare him to fire his gun.

The guard calls for help. A group of British soldiers rush to the scene. They have muskets, swords, and bayonets! They look ready to use them.

You run up the street and around the corner, then turn around to look back. Snowballs fly toward the soldiers. The soldiers yell threats as they try to keep the crowd back. You see a club fly through the air and knock someone down. Then you hear a terrible sound. One of the British guns shoots into the crowd. You freeze for a moment, but when you hear more shots, you run for home.

From your warm bed, you hear your father telling your mother that four men lay dead on the street. Crispus Attucks, a free black man, was the first to fall. Other men are wounded.

The next day, your neighbors are sad and angry. They can't believe the soldiers fired their guns. A few days later, you learn that a fifth man died. Sam Adams is calling it a ***massacre.*** You never thought something like this would happen in your town.

What do you think?

Were there any heroes in the Boston Massacre?

Paul Revere made the picture on the right. He did it on a piece of copper so it could be printed over and over again. Revere did not show things exactly as they happened. Look at the picture and answer the questions as a class.

1. Look at the British soldiers. They are standing in a straight line. They are pointing their guns at the people. One soldier on the right is telling the others to shoot. Now look at the crowd. It is peaceful. Does this match what you have learned about the Boston Massacre?
2. How do you feel when you look at the picture?
3. How do you think Paul Revere wanted people to feel when they looked at the picture?
4. How do you think the British might have drawn the Boston Massacre?

The BLOODY MASSACRE perpetrated in King-Street
BUTCHER'S HALL
Engrav'd Printed & Sold by PAUL REVERE BOSTON
Unhappy BOSTON! see thy Sons deplore,
Thy hallow'd Walks besmear'd with guiltless Gore:
While faithless P—n and his savage Bands,
With murd'rous Rancour stretch their bloody Hands;
Like fierce Barbarians grinning o'er their Prey,
Approve the Carnage, and enjoy the Day.
If scalding drops from Rage from Anguish Wrung
If speechless Sorrows lab'ring for a Tongue,
Or if a weeping World can ought appease
The plaintive Ghosts of Victims such as these;
The Patriot's copious Tears for each are shed,
A glorious Tribute which embalms the Dead
But know, FATE summons to that awful Goal,
Where JUSTICE strips the Murd'rer of his Soul:
Should venal C—ts the scandal of the Land,
Snatch the relentless Villain from her Hand,
Keen Execrations on this Plate inscrib'd,
Shall reach a JUDGE who never can be brib'd.
The unhappy Sufferers were Mess.rs SAM.L GRAY, SAM.L MAVERICK, JAM.S CALDWELL, CRISPUS ATTUCKS & PAT.K CARR
Killed. Six wounded; two of them (CHRIST.R MONK & JOHN CLARK) Mortally
Published in 1770 by Paul Revere Boston

The Boston Tea Party

The British stopped most of the taxes. There was only one left—the tax on tea.

A group of men met at the Old South Church to talk about it. They called themselves the Sons of Liberty. Sam Adams said they should do something other than just talk.

The men marched down to the ***wharf*** where the tea ships were docked. Some men dressed up like Indians. They split into groups and boarded the ships.

First they took the captain and crew below deck. Then they cracked open the heavy chests of tea and dumped them into the water. They ruined thousands of dollars worth of tea that night.

The British were angry. They wanted to punish the colonists. They closed the port of Boston until the people paid for the spoiled tea. No ships with goods to sell could move in or out of the harbor. Boston was a busy trading city. Closing the port really hurt the people.

Teamwork!

The colonists decided to work together. They wrote letters back and forth. People in Massachusetts wrote to people in Virginia. People in North Carolina wrote to people in New York. They told each other what was happening in their colonies.

Leaders from all the colonies met to talk about their problems with England. This was called the First Continental Congress. A ***congress*** is a group of representatives who meet to work out a problem.

Patriots and Loyalists

Some of the colonists wanted to break away from England and rule themselves as a new country. They wanted ***independence.*** They were called ***Patriots.***

No one wanted to think that all this might lead to war. But the Patriots started to say they would do whatever it took to be free.

Other colonists just wanted the British to stop the taxes and go home. They were called ***Loyalists*** because they were loyal to England. They did not want to go to war.

What do you think?

- By working together, the colonists could do more. Have you ever used teamwork to get something done? Did it make the job easier?
- Would you have been a Patriot or a Loyalist? What would you have done if your family did not agree with your choice?

"Other young men like myself . . . joined in. . . . The chests were . . . opened, the tea emptied over the side, and the chests thrown overboard. . . .
Although there were many people on the wharf, [there was] no talking. Nothing was [touched] but the teas. . . . the deck was swept clean and everything put in its proper place. An officer on board was [asked] to come up from the cabin and see that no damage was done except to the tea."
—Robert Sessions' diary

Minutemen left their plows and got ready to fight for freedom.

Getting Ready

The people of Massachusetts decided to get ready for war—just in case. They set up militia units. They collected guns, bullets, and other weapons. They kept them in the town of Concord.

They asked young men to sign up to fight. Some would be ***minutemen.*** The minutemen would be the first to go and fight if there was trouble. They had to be ready in just a few minutes. If they were out plowing their fields, they had to stop, get their guns, bullets, and powder, and rush off to battle. Someone else would have to take over the plowing.

Lesson 1

Memory Master

1. What is a revolution?
2. Why were the colonists upset about the taxes?
3. What was the Boston Tea Party?

Lesson 2

"The British Are Coming!"

What would you do if you were a Patriot and you found out the British wanted to steal your weapons and hurt your friends? Maybe you would be brave enough to do what Paul Revere did.

The Fighting Begins

PEOPLE TO KNOW
John Adams
William Dawes
King George
John Hancock
Thomas Jefferson
Samuel Prescott
Paul Revere

PLACES TO LOCATE
Philadelphia, Pennsylvania
Martha's Vineyard
Boston
Bunker Hill
Cambridge
Charlestown
Concord
Gloucester
Lexington
New Bedford

WORDS TO UNDERSTAND
declaration
inalienable
trench

This statue of Paul Revere is in Boston. Read on to learn why it stands near the Old North Church.

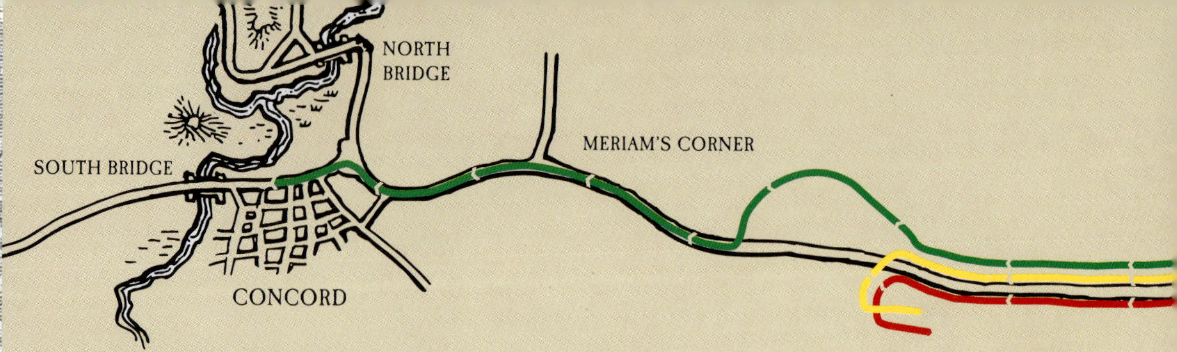

Brave Paul Revere

Paul Revere was working as an express rider for the Patriots. It was his job to carry news and messages to other places. This was an important job in the 1700s. There were no telephones, radios, or computers.

One April night, Revere was told to ride to Lexington. He had to warn Sam Adams and John Hancock that British troops were coming to arrest them. The two men were hiding in Lexington. Paul Revere had to warn the people that there might be trouble.

Which way would the troops march? Would they go by land, or take the shortcut by sea and then march the rest of the way? Could Paul Revere make it there before they did?

Paul Revere set up a signal to tell the militia which way the British would go. In the bell tower of the Old North Church, one lantern would shine if the British went by land. Two lanterns would shine if they went by sea.

In the dark of the night, Paul Revere waited and watched. Soon he saw two lanterns glowing in the Old North Church.

Some friends rowed him across the river to Charlestown. Then he climbed onto "Brown Beauty" and rode into the night.

Another rider, William Dawes, had left the other side of Boston with the same task. At each village and farm they passed, they shouted their message—the British were coming!

Revere and Dawes met at Lexington. They decided to ride on and warn the people of Concord. They wanted to protect the supplies that the colonists were hiding there. A third rider went with them. His name was Dr. Samuel Prescott.

But wait! Some British guards stopped the three riders. First Prescott escaped! Then Dawes escaped! The British kept Paul Revere for a few hours, then they let him go. He was there to see what happened the next morning in Lexington.

Robert Newman crept through the dark empty church to hang two lanterns in the tower. The lanterns were a signal that the British were coming by sea. Revere then rode to tell the people in Lexington and Concord to get ready. The British were coming!

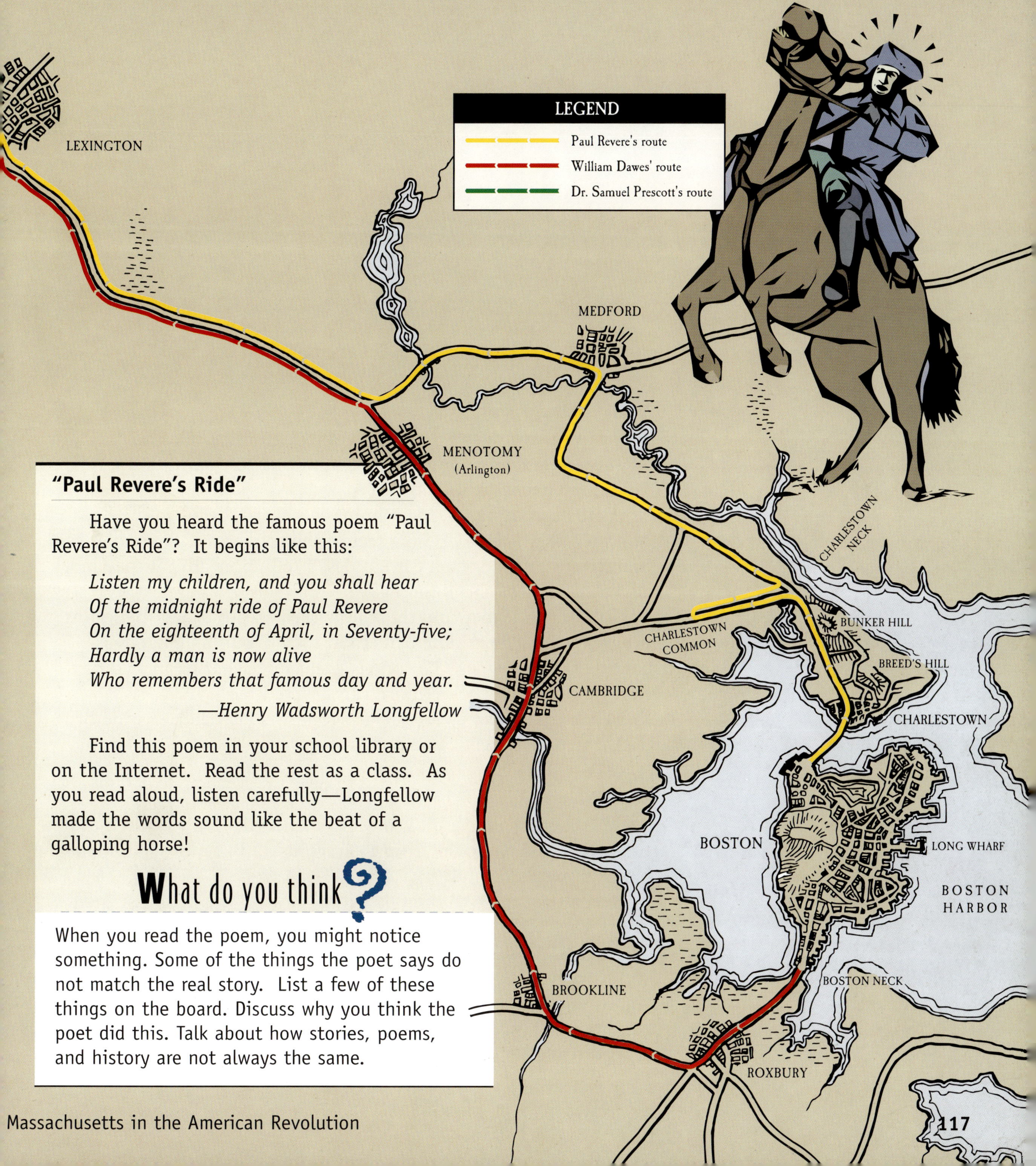

"Paul Revere's Ride"

Have you heard the famous poem "Paul Revere's Ride"? It begins like this:

Listen my children, and you shall hear
Of the midnight ride of Paul Revere
On the eighteenth of April, in Seventy-five;
Hardly a man is now alive
Who remembers that famous day and year.

—*Henry Wadsworth Longfellow*

Find this poem in your school library or on the Internet. Read the rest as a class. As you read aloud, listen carefully—Longfellow made the words sound like the beat of a galloping horse!

What do you think?

When you read the poem, you might notice something. Some of the things the poet says do not match the real story. List a few of these things on the board. Discuss why you think the poet did this. Talk about how stories, poems, and history are not always the same.

The Battles of Lexington and Concord took place on April 19, 1775. April 19th is now a state holiday called Patriot's Day. How do you celebrate Patriot's Day?

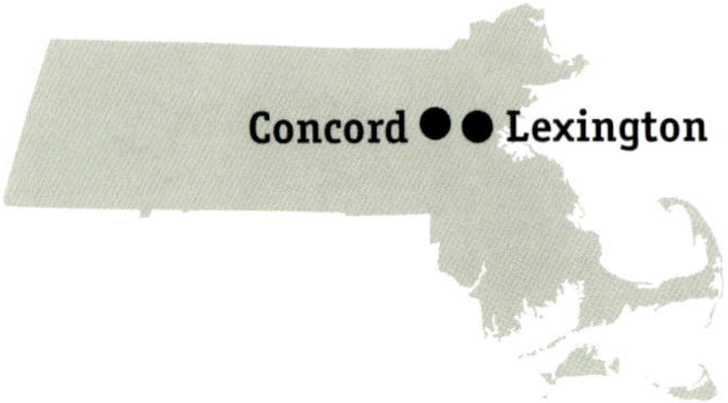

Lexington

The British soldiers marched to Lexington and Concord. Thanks to Paul Revere, the minutemen were waiting for them on the Lexington Green.

As the sun came up, the minutemen heard drums in the distance. Soon they heard the marching feet of the soldiers. Their leader said, "Stand your ground. Don't fire unless fired upon. But if they mean to have a war let it begin here!"

The British leader told the minutemen to put down their guns and go home. The minutemen stood their ground. There was shouting on both sides. No one is quite sure what happened next, but a shot rang out. Soon more shots were fired.

When the smoke cleared, eight colonists lay dead. As the British left, the people slowly came out to the green.

Concord

The British soldiers moved on to Concord. They wanted to take gunpowder and weapons from the colonists. But more minutemen were waiting there.

When they came to the Old North Bridge, the British started firing. The colonists shot back. Later, a poet named Ralph Waldo Emerson called it "the shot heard round the world." The colonists fired from behind trees, barns, and stone walls. The British were not used to this kind of fighting. They did not know which way to turn and shoot. They were worn out from their long march. Finally, they stopped firing.

Battle of Bunker Hill

The British slowly made their way back to Boston. Just across the river was Bunker Hill. The colonists began digging into the hill to make ***trenches.*** The British would have to climb the hill to attack.

Rows and rows of British soldiers climbed up the hill. The colonists did not have much gunpowder, so they had to make it last. Their leader told them, "Don't fire until you see the whites of their eyes!"

A soldier carried this bullet box into battle. It probably had a strap sewn onto it at the time.

When the British got to the top of the hill, the colonists started firing. All at once, the hill was full of smoke. Bullets flew everywhere.

The British kept coming. They finally captured the hill, but they had lost many men. The colonists had lost men too, but not nearly as many. The Battle of Bunker Hill showed the British that the colonists could stand and fight very well.

Other Battles in Massachusetts

There were raids and battles in other Massachusetts towns, such as Cambridge, Gloucester, New Bedford, and Martha's Vineyard. After about a year, the fighting moved to other colonies.

YOUR TOWN

Does your town have any Revolutionary War history? Call or visit your historical society to find out:

- Were there any battles in or near your town?
- Are there any soldiers from that time buried in your town's cemetery?
- Does your town have any monuments to the Patriots?
- Did your town have a newspaper during that time?

The British charged up Bunker Hill.

The Declaration of Independence

More and more colonists wanted independence. Leaders met again in Philadelphia. (This time, the meeting was called the Second Continental Congress.) The leaders agreed to break away from England and start their own country.

They decided to send a letter to the whole world. They called the letter a ***declaration.*** A declaration makes something known to everyone. It is like an announcement. Who could write such an important letter?

Who Will Write the Declaration?

A lot of people thought John Adams should write it. He was a very smart Patriot from Massachusetts. Adams did not think he was the best one to write it. He thought a man from Virginia named Thomas Jefferson should write it. Jefferson said he would try his best.

What Does It Say?

Thomas Jefferson worked hard to find the best words to use. He wrote in a way that showed common sense. He said the colonists were going to explain why they wanted to be free:

- They have rights that cannot be taken away. They believe "that all men are created equal, that they are endowed by their Creator with certain ***inalienable*** Rights, that among these are Life, Liberty, and the pursuit of Happiness."
- A government should protect these rights.
- If the government does not protect them, then the people can start a new government.
- Governments get their power from the people.
- The British government and the king have hurt the colonists. Jefferson listed the ways.
- The colonists were right to go to war. They were right because the British had harmed them instead of protecting them.

Spreading the News

On July 4, 1776, the Declaration of Independence was approved. The Congress printed copies of it. Riders carried copies to all the colonies.

In Boston, the Declaration was read from the balcony of the Old State House. The people listened in the street below.

The First to Sign

About a month later, the Declaration was ready to sign. It was copied onto special paper. John Hancock was the first to sign it. He walked up to the table and wrote his name in very large letters. He said, "There! [Britain] can read my name without spectacles, and may now double the reward. . . ." Look for his name at the bottom of the Declaration.

One by one, the rest of the leaders signed the Declaration of Independence.

The states were on their way to being a new country. It was not going to be easy. They still had to fight a war.

What do you think?

- Many weeks later, across the Atlantic Ocean in England, King George got the Declaration of Independence. What do you think he thought when he read it?
- How would you have felt if you were in the crowd in front of the Old State House, hearing it for the first time?

It All Started Here

The Revolution began right here in Massachusetts. Boston was the center of the action. If you follow the Freedom Trail, you can see places where history was made. Here are a few of the things you can see.

1

*The people gathered at **"Old South"** to hold town meetings and protest the British laws. This was where they met right before the Boston Tea Party.*

2

*Sam Adams, John Hancock, and Paul Revere are buried at **Granary Burying Ground**. So are the five people killed in the Boston Massacre.*

3

*You probably know **Faneuil Hall.** A merchant named Peter Faneuil built it long ago. The first floor was a marketplace. It had stalls where people could buy meat, vegetables, and other things they needed each day. The second floor had meeting rooms. It became the town hall. People came to talk about ideas and choose town leaders.*

Lesson 2

Memory Master

1. Why is Paul Revere famous today?
2. What is a minuteman?
3. Where did the first battles of the American Revolution take place?
4. What was the Declaration of Independence? When was it approved by the Patriot leaders?

*This is the **Bunker Hill Monument**. It marks the place where the Battle of Bunker Hill was fought. It helps us remember the people who fought for freedom.*

*This is the **Old State House**. The Declaration of Independence was read to the people of Boston from its balcony.*

Lesson 3

Famous Patriots

PEOPLE TO KNOW
Abigail Adams
John Adams
Samuel Adams
Benjamin Franklin
John Hancock
Paul Revere
Deborah Samson
George Washington
Phillis Wheatley

PLACES TO LOCATE
Pennsylvania
Boston
Quincy

WORDS TO UNDERSTAND
almanac
boycott
engraving
opinion
pamphlet
politics
publish
rights

Ben Franklin

1706–1790

What do you know about Benjamin Franklin? You may know that he discovered lightning was electricity. He did much more than that. Read on to find out why he is so famous today.

Young Ben

Ben Franklin was the 15th child in his family. His father was a soap and candle maker in Boston. Because his family was very poor, young Ben only went to school for about two years.

Ben was a bright boy who loved to read. When he looked for his first job, he went to his brother James. James ran a printing shop. He made Ben an apprentice.

Ben the Printer

Ben quickly learned the printing trade. He did not get along well with his brother, and he ran away from Boston. He went to Pennsylvania and worked for another printer. Before long, he set up his own print shop.

Ben the Writer

Ben loved to write. He bought a newspaper business. He wrote many funny stories for the newspaper. Readers liked his sense of humor. Ben also wrote and printed a book that made him famous. It was called *Poor Richard's Almanac*.

An ***almanac*** is a book that tells about the weather, ocean tides, and the movement of the sun, stars, and moon. Farmers used the almanac to learn when to plant their crops. The almanac also had good advice like, "A plowman on his legs is higher than a gentleman on his horse." What do you think he meant by that?

Before long, Franklin's almanac was read in every colony. People in Europe were reading it too. The almanac made Ben rich and famous. He did not have to work for money anymore. Now he could spend time on his hobbies.

Ben the Scientist

Ben loved to do experiments. His most famous experiment was with electricity. He tied a metal key onto a kite. He flew the kite during a storm. When lightning struck the key, it made a spark. Ben proved that lightning was electricity.

After spending a cold night at an inn, Ben went to work on a way to keep a whole room warm. He invented the Franklin stove. It sent the warm air back into the room instead of up the chimney.

Ben Franklin also started the first lending library. People who could not afford to buy books could borrow them. We also owe him thanks for street paving, street lighting, street cleaning, police and fire departments, bifocal glasses, the lightning rod, the best cure for a cold (sleep, good diet, and fresh air), and a plan for uniting the colonies.

Ben the Leader

Benjamin Franklin wanted his country to be free from England. He worked with the other Patriots. He signed the Declaration of Independence. After the war, he helped Pennsylvania plan its new government. He also helped write the United States Constitution.

"From a child I was fond of reading, and all the little money that came into my hands was ever laid out in books."

—Benjamin Franklin

Samuel Adams

1722–1803

Samuel Adams was a true Patriot. He spoke up for the ***rights*** *of the colonists. He said the colonies should break away from England. He became a very important leader.*

Young Samuel

Sam Adams was born in Boston. He went to the Boston Latin School. Then he went to Harvard.

Sam tried many jobs. He studied law for a while. He worked for a merchant. He tried becoming a brewer (a person who makes ale, or beer).

Then he found something he did very well. He was working as the tax collector of Boston. He had strong ideas and ***opinions*** about the taxes. He did not think the taxes were fair. He was not shy about speaking up, and he was a good speaker. He believed what he said, and it showed. He found out he was very good at ***politics.***

A Proud Patriot and Leader

People listened to Sam Adams. They started to look to him as a leader.

Sam worked day and night for his country. He:

- led protests and ***boycotts***
- started the Sons of Liberty
- led the Boston Tea Party
- represented the people of Boston in the General Court
- wrote in ***pamphlets*** and newspapers
- gave speeches that made people want liberty
- told leaders of all of the colonies to meet (the meeting was called the Continental Congress)
- was a member of the First Continental Congress
- was a member of the Second Continental Congress
- signed the Declaration of Independence
- helped write a state constitution for Massachusetts
- helped get Massachusetts to agree to the U.S. Constitution
- served as lieutenant (assistant) governor of Massachusetts
- served as governor of Massachusetts for four years

Paul Revere

1734–1818

One of the most famous people from this time is Paul Revere. We know him for his midnight ride, but there was much more to his life.

A Skilled Craftsman

Paul Revere was born in Boston. His father taught him how to make things out of gold and silver. When his father died, Paul had to take care of the family.

Paul Revere became a good silversmith. He made silver bowls, pitchers, knives, forks, spoons, and tea sets to sell. He did some other jobs too. He made copper ***engravings.*** He also worked as a dentist. He gave people false teeth made out of ivory or animal teeth.

Family Life

Paul married Sarah Orne, and they had eight children. After she died, he married Rachel Walker. They also had eight children. Some of them died, but the Revere house was always full of children.

Making History

Paul Revere was working for Patriot leaders as an express rider. He carried messages back and forth. When the Boston Tea Party happened, he spread the word. He galloped to New York and Philadelphia to tell the people there.

One spring night, his job was to ride to Lexington with a very important message. What was the message? The British were coming! He rode all night to warn John Hancock and Sam Adams. As he rode, he warned people across the countryside. The rest is history.

Most of the famous men you have read about in this chapter did not fight in the war. They were very important in other ways, but they were not soldiers. Paul Revere did fight in the war. He had fought the French and Indians before, so he knew what war was like. If you could ask him a question about it, what would it be?

After the War

After the war, Paul made bells and cannons to sell. He started the first copper mill in America. It was in Canton. He also printed money for Massachusetts.

When Paul Revere died, he left his business to his sons. You can visit his grave at Granary Burying Ground in Boston.

John Adams

1735–1826

John Adams was Sam Adams' cousin. John was important before the first battle of the American Revolution and long after the war ended. Later, he became the second president of the United States.

Adams' farm in Braintree

Early Life

John Adams was born in Braintree in an area that is now part of Quincy. He grew up on his family's farm, and had a horse named Cleopatra.

When he was old enough, John Adams went to Harvard. He taught school, then decided to study law. He became a great lawyer.

True Love

John fell in love with Abigail Smith. Like him, she loved to read and think. They were married and had children. One of them, John Quincy, would become the sixth president of the United States.

John's work took him away from home a lot. He and Abigail wrote wonderful letters to each other. They shared news and ideas. They talked about all that was happening in the colonies.

A Man of Ideas

Adams wanted the colonies to be free. He argued against the Stamp Act. He got other men to sign a paper saying why the act was unfair.

He always tried to be fair. Remember the British soldiers who fired their guns during the Boston Massacre? Adams was their lawyer in court. He did not like what they did, but he believed that everyone—even British soldiers—should get a fair trial.

The British knew John Adams was smart. They knew he could do great things. They tried to get him to switch to their side. They said they would pay him a lot of money to come and work for them. Adams said no. He wanted freedom more than money.

Other Patriots looked up to John Adams. They sent him to the General Court. They sent him to both the First and Second Continental Congresses.

At the meetings, Adams was full of good ideas. He was one of the first men to say the colonies should be independent. He also made two great choices. One was that George Washington should lead the American troops. The other was that Thomas Jefferson should write the Declaration of Independence.

Helping the New Country

John Adams did not stop working after the war was won. He went to Europe to represent his new country. He helped make the treaty that ended the war. He helped decide where his new country's boundaries would be.

Back at home, he wrote a state constitution for Massachusetts. He became the first vice president of the United States. (George Washington was the first president.) Then Adams was chosen to be president.

Our Second President

John Adams was the second president of the United States. At that time, the White House was just being built. Adams was the first president to live in it. On his first night sleeping there, he wrote a letter to his wife. He wrote, "May none but honest and wise Men ever rule under this roof."

Back at the Farm

After being president, John went home to the family farm. He and Abigail were happy there. He had given all he could to form a free country. He died on July 4, 1826. That was exactly 50 years after the Declaration of Independence was signed. Thomas Jefferson died on the same day.

John Hancock

John Hancock

1737–1793

Look at the bottom of the Declaration of Independence. Whose name stands out? John Hancock's! He was the first to sign it. He helped move the colonists toward freedom.

Young John

When John Hancock was just a boy, his father died. John's uncle took care of him. His uncle was a rich merchant who had no children.

John went to Harvard, then worked for his uncle. When his uncle died, he left his fortune to John.

With all this money, John could have chosen to sit back and ignore the problems of the people. He did not. He got to know Sam Adams and some of the other Patriots. He believed the same things they believed about freedom. He wanted the same things they wanted. He cheered the Boston Tea Party. He helped move the colonists toward revolution.

A Proud Leader

The British knew John Hancock was a strong leader. They knew he was buying guns for the Patriots. They wanted to arrest him. Hancock knew the British were looking for him. They would give a reward to anyone who would catch him. He was hiding in Lexington during the first battles of the war.

John Hancock went on to lead the Continental Congresses. He was not afraid to sign the Declaration of Independence. He said, "There! [Britain] can read that name without spectacles, and may now double the reward . . . for my head."

Our First Governor

When the people of Massachusetts chose their first governor, they picked John Hancock. The State House was built on land that belonged to him. The State House is where our state government meets today.

When people today sign something, they often say they are "putting their John Hancock on it."

Phillis Wheatley

1753?–1784

*Phillis Wheatley went from being a slave to being a poet. She was the first African American to **publish** a book of poems. Here is her story.*

A Young Slave

When Phillis Wheatley was eight years old, she was brought to Boston as a slave. Phillis was not her real name. Most slaves did not get to keep their real names. Once they got to America, they were given new names. *Phillis* was the name of the slave ship that brought her to America. Her last name, Wheatley, was from the man who bought her. His name was John Wheatley.

It did not take long for Phillis to learn English. She was very smart. She learned to read the Bible very well.

The Wheatleys saw how smart the little girl was. They let her study. She learned Latin and read poetry. She only had to do a little bit of work around the house. The rest of the time she could read and write poems.

A Young Poet

Phillis' first poem was published when she was only 14. Later, she published a book of poems. Mr. Wheatley freed her that same year.

People began to know Phillis Wheatley's name. She traveled to England to talk about her book. She helped many people see that African Americans should be treated better. She even sent George Washington a letter with a poem in it. She called him the "great chief." Washington wrote back to her. He said she was a good poet, and he would like to meet her someday.

A Sad Ending

Phillis married John Peters, and they had three children. Soon her happy days turned sad. When her husband left her and the children, they became very poor. Two of her children died. Just a few hours after Phillis died, her third child died.

Proceed, great chief, with virtue on thy side,
Thy ev'ry action let the goddess guide.
A crown, a mansion, and a throne that shine,
With gold unfading, WASHINGTON! be thine.

—Phillis Wheatley,
from her poem to General George Washington

In the poem, the "goddess" is Columbia, a woman who was a symbol of America. At the time, Columbia was in many poems and paintings.

Phillis Wheatley's book was called Poems on Various Subjects, Religious and Moral. This picture was on the cover. ▶

PHILLIS WHEATLEY, NEGRO SERVANT to Mr. JOHN WHEATLEY, of BOSTON.
Phillis Wheatley

Abigail Adams

1744–1818

Abigail Adams was a Patriot and first lady. She was the wife of the second president of the United States, John Adams. She was also the mother of the sixth president of the United States, John Quincy Adams.

Abigail Smith was from Weymouth. She did not get to go to school, but she was very smart. She loved to read.

Abigail married John Adams. She called him her "dearest friend." They lived at his farm in Braintree (now Quincy) and in Boston. They had three sons and two daughters. One of the girls died at birth. One of their boys, John Quincy, became president of the United States.

While John was busy with his work, Abigail was busy at home. She had to keep the farm running. When her children were not in school, she taught them lessons herself.

In those days, women had few rights. They could not vote. Few women owned land. Slaves had no rights at all. Abigail believed that women should have rights. She told her husband to "remember the ladies." She said the men should think of women and slaves in all their talk of freedom.

When John became vice president, Abigail held dinners for many people. She became good friends with Martha Washington. When John became president, she went to live with him in Washington, D.C. After that, they went home to Quincy.

Deborah Samson

1760–1827

Do you remember reading about Deborah Samson in Chapter 1? She is our state heroine. That means we remember and honor what she did for our state.

Deborah Samson wanted to help win the war. Women were not allowed to fight then, so she dressed up as a man. She signed her name as Robert Shirtliff. She was a brave soldier.

After the war, Deborah was poor. The government gave her money. She was the first soldier to get money from the government. It was the country's way of saying thank you.

Many years after she died, Deborah Samson became the state heroine of Massachusetts.

Memory Master

Lesson 3

1. Name one thing for which Benjamin Franklin is famous.
2. ________ ________ led the Boston Tea Party.
3. The first governor of the state of Massachusetts was ________ ________.
4. ________ ________ was the first African American to publish a book of poems.
5. Abigail Adams told her husband, John Adams, to "Remember the ________."

Lesson 4

A New Nation

PEOPLE TO KNOW
John Adams
Betsy Ross

PLACES TO LOCATE
France
Yorktown, Virginia

WORDS TO UNDERSTAND
amend
constellation
criticize
document
privacy
state
surrender

Results of the Revolution

John Adams told the colonies that other countries might help fight the British. France sent ships, soldiers, and supplies. With France's help, the colonists won the war.

The British did not think the colonists could win. The Americans won many battles. The last important one was at Yorktown, Virginia. The British finally had to ***surrender.***

The colonies were now free ***states.*** Each state had already set up a government of its own. What would hold the states together?

Government for the People

During the American Revolution, the leaders planned a government for the nation. They wrote rules for the new government. But after the war ended, many leaders thought the new country needed a stronger government. In 1787, they wrote the Constitution.

The Constitution

Our government is based on our Constitution. Here are some of its main points:

- The people run the government. We vote for who we want to represent us. We vote for who we want to lead us.
- The Constitution is the highest law of the land.
- Power is divided among the president, the Congress, and the courts.
- The people can change, or ***amend,*** the Constitution.
- There will be an army to defend America in case of war.
- The president will lead the army.

What do the first three words of the Constitution say? What clues do those words give you about the kind of government the people wanted? ▶

We the People of the United States, in Order to form a more perfect Union, establish Justice, insure domestic Tranquility, provide for the common defence, promote the general Welfare, and secure the Blessings of Liberty to ourselves and our Posterity, do ordain and establish this Constitution for the United States of America.

Article. I.

Section. 1. All legislative Powers herein granted shall be vested in a Congress of the United States, which shall consist of a Senate and House of Representatives.

Section. 2. The House of Representatives shall be composed of Members chosen every second Year by the People of the several States, and the Electors in each State shall have the Qualifications requisite for Electors of the most numerous Branch of the State Legislature.

No Person shall be a Representative who shall not have attained to the Age of twenty five Years, and been seven Years a Citizen of the United States, and who shall not, when elected, be an Inhabitant of that State in which he shall be chosen.

Representatives and direct Taxes shall be apportioned among the several States which may be included within this Union, according to their respective Numbers, which shall be determined by adding to the whole Number of free Persons, including those bound to Service for a Term of Years, and excluding Indians not taxed, three fifths of all other Persons. The actual Enumeration shall be made within three Years after the first Meeting of the Congress of the United States, and within every subsequent Term of ten Years, in such Manner as they shall by Law direct. The Number of Representatives shall not exceed one for every thirty Thousand, but each State shall have at Least one Representative; and until such enumeration shall be made, the State of New Hampshire shall be entitled to chuse three, Massachusetts eight, Rhode Island and Providence Plantations one, Connecticut five, New York six, New Jersey four, Pennsylvania eight, Delaware one, Maryland six, Virginia ten, North Carolina five, South Carolina five, and Georgia three.

When vacancies happen in the Representation from any State, the Executive Authority thereof shall issue Writs of Election to fill such Vacancies.

The House of Representatives shall chuse their Speaker and other Officers; and shall have the sole Power of Impeachment.

Section. 3. The Senate of the United States shall be composed of two Senators from each State, chosen by the Legislature thereof for six Years; and each Senator shall have one Vote.

Immediately after they shall be assembled in Consequence of the first Election, they shall be divided as equally as may be into three Classes. The Seats of the Senators of the first Class shall be vacated at the Expiration of the second Year, of the second Class at the Expiration of the fourth Year, and of the third Class at the Expiration of the sixth Year, so that one third may be chosen every second Year; and if Vacancies happen by Resignation, or otherwise, during the Recess of the Legislature of any State, the Executive thereof may make temporary Appointments until the next Meeting of the Legislature, which shall then fill such Vacancies.

No Person shall be a Senator who shall not have attained to the Age of thirty Years, and been nine Years a Citizen of the United States, and who shall not, when elected, be an Inhabitant of that State for which he shall be chosen.

The Vice President of the United States shall be President of the Senate, but shall have no Vote, unless they be equally divided.

The Senate shall chuse their other Officers, and also a President pro tempore, in the Absence of the Vice President, or when he shall exercise the Office of President of the United States.

The Senate shall have the sole Power to try all Impeachments. When sitting for that Purpose, they shall be on Oath or Affirmation. When the President of the United States is tried, the Chief Justice shall preside: And no Person shall be convicted without the Concurrence of two thirds of the Members present.

Judgment in Cases of Impeachment shall not extend further than to removal from Office, and disqualification to hold and enjoy any Office of honor, Trust or Profit under the United States: but the Party convicted shall nevertheless be liable and subject to Indictment, Trial, Judgment and Punishment, according to Law.

Section. 4. The Times, Places and Manner of holding Elections for Senators and Representatives, shall be prescribed in each State by the Legislature thereof; but the Congress may at any time by Law make or alter such Regulations, except as to the Places of chusing Senators.

The Congress shall assemble at least once in every Year, and such Meeting shall be on the first Monday in December, unless they shall by Law appoint a different Day.

Section. 5. Each House shall be the Judge of the Elections, Returns and Qualifications of its own Members, and a Majority of each shall constitute a Quorum to do Business; but a smaller Number may adjourn from day to day, and may be authorized to compel the Attendance of absent Members, in such Manner, and under such Penalties as each House may provide.

Each House may determine the Rules of its Proceedings, punish its Members for disorderly Behaviour, and, with the Concurrence of two thirds, expel a Member.

Each House shall keep a Journal of its Proceedings, and from time to time publish the same, excepting such Parts as may in their Judgment require Secrecy; and the Yeas and Nays of the Members of either House on any question shall, at the Desire of one fifth of those Present, be entered on the Journal.

Neither House, during the Session of Congress, shall, without the Consent of the other, adjourn for more than three days, nor to any other Place than that in which the two Houses shall be sitting.

Section. 6. The Senators and Representatives shall receive a Compensation for their Services, to be ascertained by Law, and paid out of the Treasury of the United States. They shall in all Cases, except Treason, Felony and Breach of the Peace, be privileged from Arrest during their Attendance at the Session of their respective Houses, and in going to and returning from the same; and for any Speech or Debate in either House, they shall not be questioned in any other Place.

No Senator or Representative shall, during the Time for which he was elected, be appointed to any civil Office under the Authority of the United States, which shall have been created, or the Emoluments whereof shall have been encreased during such time; and no Person holding any Office under the United States, shall be a Member of either House during his Continuance in Office.

Section. 7. All Bills for raising Revenue shall originate in the House of Representatives; but the Senate may propose or concur with Amendments as on other Bills.

Every Bill which shall have passed the House of Representatives and the Senate, shall, before it become a Law, be presented to the President of the

The Bill of Rights

Many people liked the new Constitution. Some still worried that important rights might not be protected. They wanted a **document** that listed their basic rights.

A few years after the Constitution was signed, ten amendments were added to the Constitution. They are called the Bill of Rights.

The Bill of Rights says our government cannot make laws that take away our rights, such as freedom of speech or religion. Talk with your teacher and your class about other rights in the Bill of Rights.

1st Amendment:
Freedom of religion: You can worship as you wish, or not at all. The government cannot choose one religion for the whole country.

Freedom of speech: You can express your opinion about any subject without being arrested. You can even **criticize** the government, but what you say cannot cause danger or harm to others.

Freedom of the press: The government cannot tell people what they can or cannot print in newspapers or books.

Freedom of assembly: You have the right to join and meet with any group. However, you cannot commit crimes with the group.

2nd Amendment:
Right to bear arms: You can own a gun for legal activities.

3rd Amendment:
Right to not have soldiers in your home during peacetime: In the past, kings made people feed and house soldiers not only during wars, but in times of peace.

4th Amendment:
Freedom from improper search and seizure: You have a right to **privacy,** but if the police have a good reason to think you have something illegal in your home, they can get a search warrant and search your home.

5th, 6th, and 7th Amendments:
These protect you if you are accused of a crime. They include the right to a speedy trial and a trial by jury.

8th Amendment:
No cruel or unusual punishment is allowed.

9th Amendment:
People can have other rights not named in the Bill of Rights.

10th Amendment:
Much power will remain with the states. The people did not want the national government to have all the power.

A Symbol of Our Nation— The United States Flag

Betsy Ross sewed the first American flag in 1776. That was the same year the colonists signed the Declaration of Independence.

The flag was a symbol for the new country. It had 13 stars and 13 stripes. Each star and stripe stood for one of the 13 states. Why stars? The stars stood for a new ***constellation.*** It was a way of saying a new nation was born. The red of the stripes stood for the blood that was shed for freedom.

Today, our flag has 50 stars. They stand for the 50 states in our country. The flag still has 13 stripes. They remind us of the first 13 states. The flag is a symbol of who we are now and a reminder of how our country began.

O say, does that star-spangled
banner yet wave
O'er the land of the free and the
home of the brave?

—"The Star-Spangled Banner,"
our national anthem

Handle With Respect

There are rules about how to use the flag. The rules help people show respect for the flag and all it stands for. Here are some of the rules:

- Never let the flag touch the ground.
- Fly the flag between sunrise and sunset. If it is flown at night, it should have lights shining on it.
- When you see the flag raised, lowered, or carried in a parade, stand up and put your hand over your heart.
- When state flags fly next to it, the United States flag should be flown higher. If the flags of other countries are flown with it, the flags should be at the same level. They should also be about the same size.
- Sometimes after someone dies, the flag is flown at half staff. To get it there, raise it all the way first, then lower it halfway. At the end of the day, raise it all the way again, then lower it all the way.
- Always let the flag hang freely.

What do you think?

Do you have a United States flag in your classroom? Have you ever walked behind the flag in a parade? How does it make you feel? What does our country mean to you?

Folding the American Flag

1. Hold the flag straight across, about waist-high.

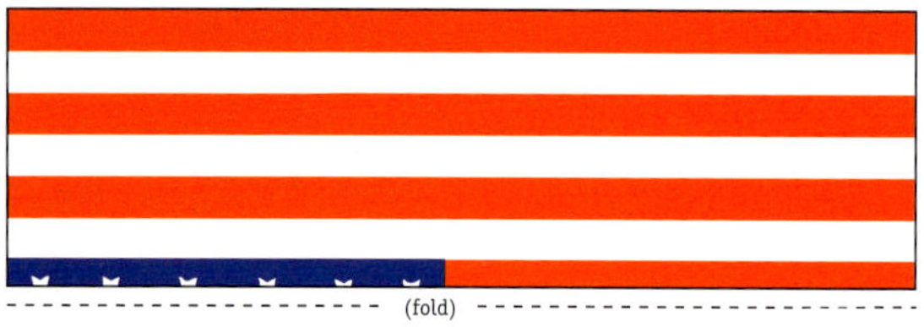

2. Fold the flag in half the long way.

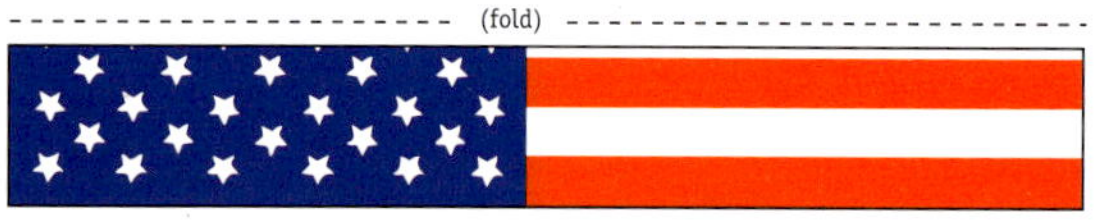

3. Fold it in half again the long way.

4. Starting at the striped end, fold up a triangle.

5. Repeat the triangles until only a triangle of blue with stars shows. Tuck in the folds.

Folding the Flag

Did you know that when the flag is taken down it is always folded in a special way? It is folded into a triangle. Why? That was the shape of the hats worn by colonial soldiers.

It takes two people to fold a flag the right way. Follow the pictures to see how it is done.

Lesson 4

Memory Master

1. What document is the basis for our nation's government today?
2. What are the first three words of the U.S. Constitution?
3. How does the United States flag stand for both our history and our nation today?

Chapter 6 Review

What's the Point?

The 13 colonies decided to break away from England. Massachusetts was a leader in the American Revolution. The first battles were at Lexington and Concord. The colonists declared independence and fought for their freedom.

After many hard battles, the colonists defeated the British. Their dream of independence had come true.

The new country built a government for the people. The leaders wrote the Constitution and Bill of Rights. They created the flag as a symbol for the new nation.

Activity

Act It Out!

Divide your class into groups. Have each group act out a stanza (section) of "Paul Revere's Ride" by Henry Wadsworth Longfellow. Practice first, then act out the poem in order from start to finish. Read the last stanza together.

"The history of every country begins in the heart of a man or a woman."

—Willa Cather

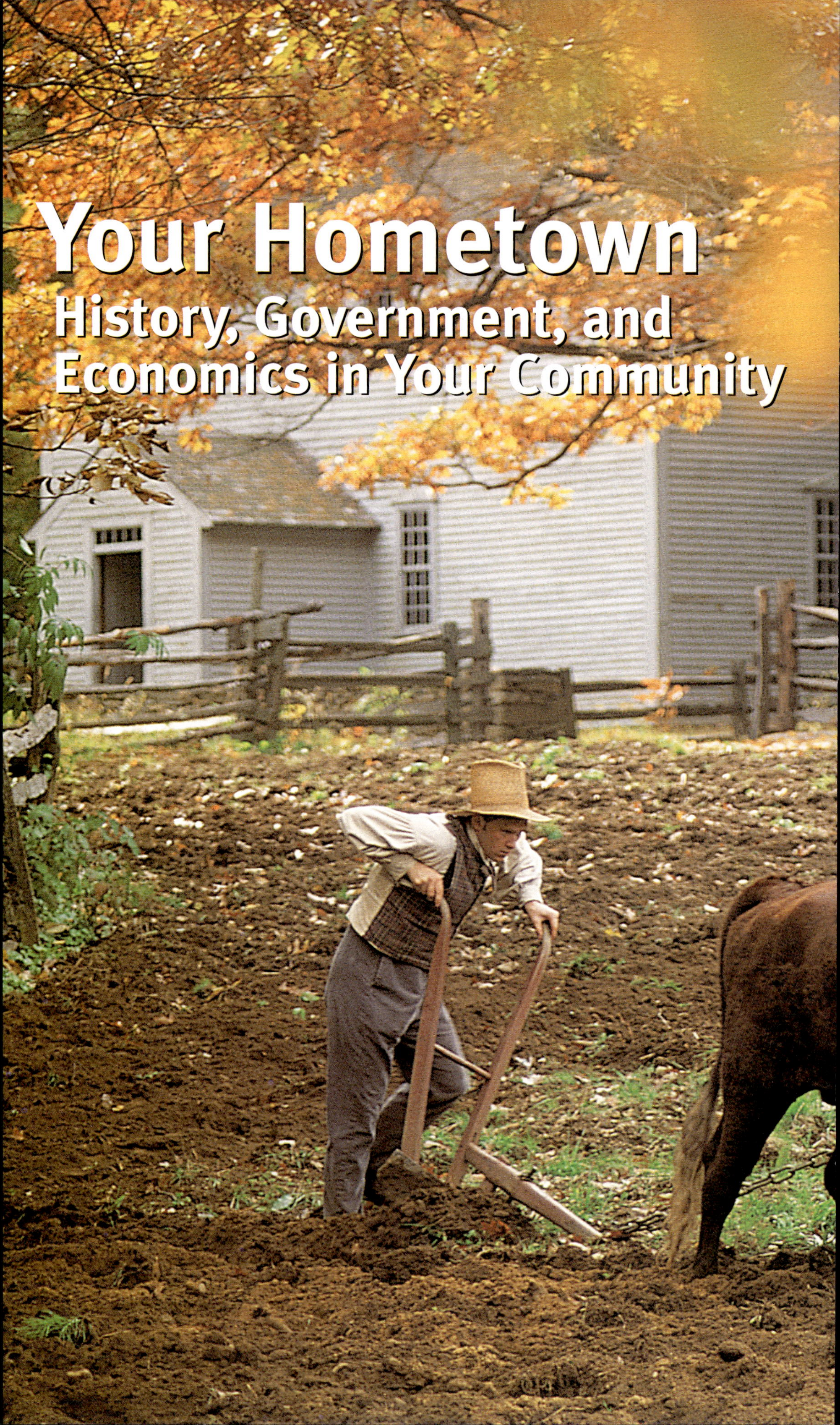

Your Hometown

History, Government, and Economics in Your Community

Chapter 7

There are many places in our state where you can learn about the past. Old Sturbridge Village is one place. You can see men plowing fields, people milking cows, blacksmiths making tools, and women dying yarn.

What places can you visit to learn about the history of your town?

Photo ©Kindra Clineff

Lesson 1

Your Town in History

WORDS TO UNDERSTAND
landmark
tradition
unique

The Hancock Shaker Village near Pittsfield shows what life was like for a group of people called the Shakers.

Each Town Has a Story

How many towns and cities are there in Massachusetts? Did you guess 100? 200? 300? There are over 350 towns and cities in our state. Each one is different from the others.

Different geography: As you learned in Chapter 1, places have different kinds of land. Some are in a river valley. Others are in the mountains. Some towns are near the ocean. Others are not next to any water.

Different people: Each town has a different mix of people. Busy cities have people from many cultures. The people have different foods and churches. Some even speak different languages. They do many different things for a living.

Different history: All towns did not start at the same time. They did not start for the same reasons. Each town has its own story.

You can see your town's history in its landmarks. A ***landmark*** is something that stands out in your town. It may be something in nature, like a mountain or a cliff. It could be something made by people, like a bridge or a statue. A landmark sets your town apart from other places.

The Cape Ann Light Station is a landmark in Rockport. A house called Arrowhead is a landmark in Pittsfield. A writer named Herman Melville wrote a famous book there. The book is called *Moby Dick*.

Plymouth Rock is a famous landmark in Plymouth. It is said to be the rock on which the Pilgrims first stepped ashore. Plymouth Rock is a landmark for our country too. It is a symbol of freedom for our nation.

Many towns in Massachusetts have museums. They tell the story of the town and of important people from the past. These children are visiting the Lynn Museum. They are learning about exciting ways the town of Lynn grew.

Activity

Visit a Cemetery

Did you ever look for history in a cemetery? Cemeteries can tell you a lot about history. Visit your town's oldest cemetery. See if you can find the oldest grave. How old is it? What century is it from? Who is buried in it? What can you learn about the person's life? What can you learn about the past? You may want to make a rubbing of the stone.

Are there any soldiers buried there? Which wars did they fight in? Find out more about the wars in which they fought.

YOUR TOWN

Your Town's Story

What makes your town ***unique,*** or different from all the others? What is your town's story?

Look on the Internet to see if your town has a website. Visit your local historical society or a nearby historic site. See if you can learn how your town got started.

- When was your town founded?
- How did it get its name?
- What are the landmarks in your town?
- What do the landmarks tell others about your town?

This woman is holding a piece of the first cable that sent messages across the Atlantic Ocean. The artifact is part of the history of Stockbridge.

Photo ©Kindra Clineff

Activity

In the Neighborhood

Who are the people in your town? Do a report on the different neighborhoods there. Here are some questions to get you started. You can think of your own questions too.

- Where are the people from?
- Do some people speak a different language?
- What are some ***traditions*** of the people?
- Look at the names of the streets. Are any of the streets named for people or events in the past?
- Talk to an older person. Ask how your neighborhood has changed over time.

Activity

Treasure Hunt

We're going on a treasure hunt! It starts at a local museum or historical society. The treasure? Artifacts! See how many you can find. What do they tell you about life in the past? What do they tell you about your town?

This drawing shows the town of Salem as it looked over 300 years ago. What looks different today?

Change Through Time

Your town was not always like it is today. People moved in and out. Stores opened and closed. New buildings went up. Old buildings were torn down.

Today there are cars and buses on the streets of your town. Long ago, people did not have these things. How did they get around? The first people in your town probably walked a lot. They rode a horse or traveled in a carriage pulled by a horse. If the people lived near water, they rode on steamboats or sailing ships. Later, they traveled on trains. Then they had cars. The first cars looked very different from the cars you see today. Have you ever seen a picture of an old car?

Activity

Pictures of the Past

You can learn a lot from an old picture. Compare these pictures to see how the State House has changed over time.

The picture on the left shows the State House being built (1795-1797). It was built on Beacon Hill. Look closely, and answer the questions.

1. What are the workers doing?
2. Why do you think they cut into the hill to build the State House?
3. Are there any other buildings around the State House?
4. Is this a drawing or a photograph? How do you know?
5. Does anything in the picture tell you how people got around during that time?

Now look at the picture on the right. It shows the State House today.

6. Look at the dome on top of the State House. Compare it to the dome on the left. Do you think the domes were made of the same material? If you said no, you were right! The first dome was made of wood. Then copper was added. Later it was covered with a layer of gold.
7. What kinds of buildings are around the State House today?
8. Is there anything in this picture that shows how people get around today?
9. Do you see the trees across the street? Why do you think there were no trees in the first picture?
10. Do you see anything else that is different from the first picture?

Activity

Compare an Old Map to a Current Map

You can see how your town has changed by looking at maps. For example, look at these two maps of Northborough. The map below is from the 19th century. The map on the right is from today. Use the maps to answer the questions.

1. What kinds of things does the old map show? Describe them as a class.
2. What kinds of things does the current map show?
3. List some things that are different on the two maps.
4. Is anything the same?
5. Do you see any bodies of water on the old map? On the current map?
6. What do you think the first map was used for?
7. What do you think the current map is used for?

See if you can find a map of your town from the 19th century. (Remember, the 19th century is the 1800s.) Answer these same questions as you study the map.

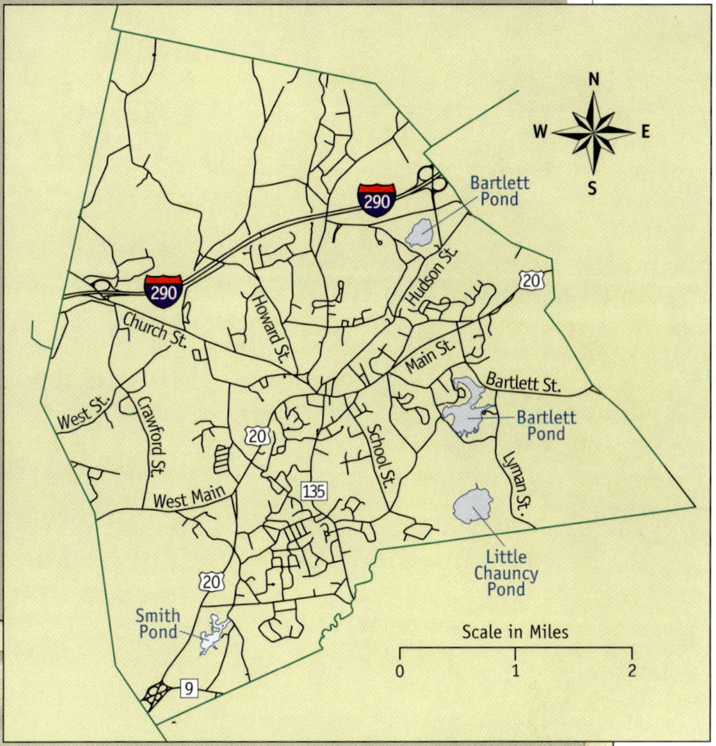

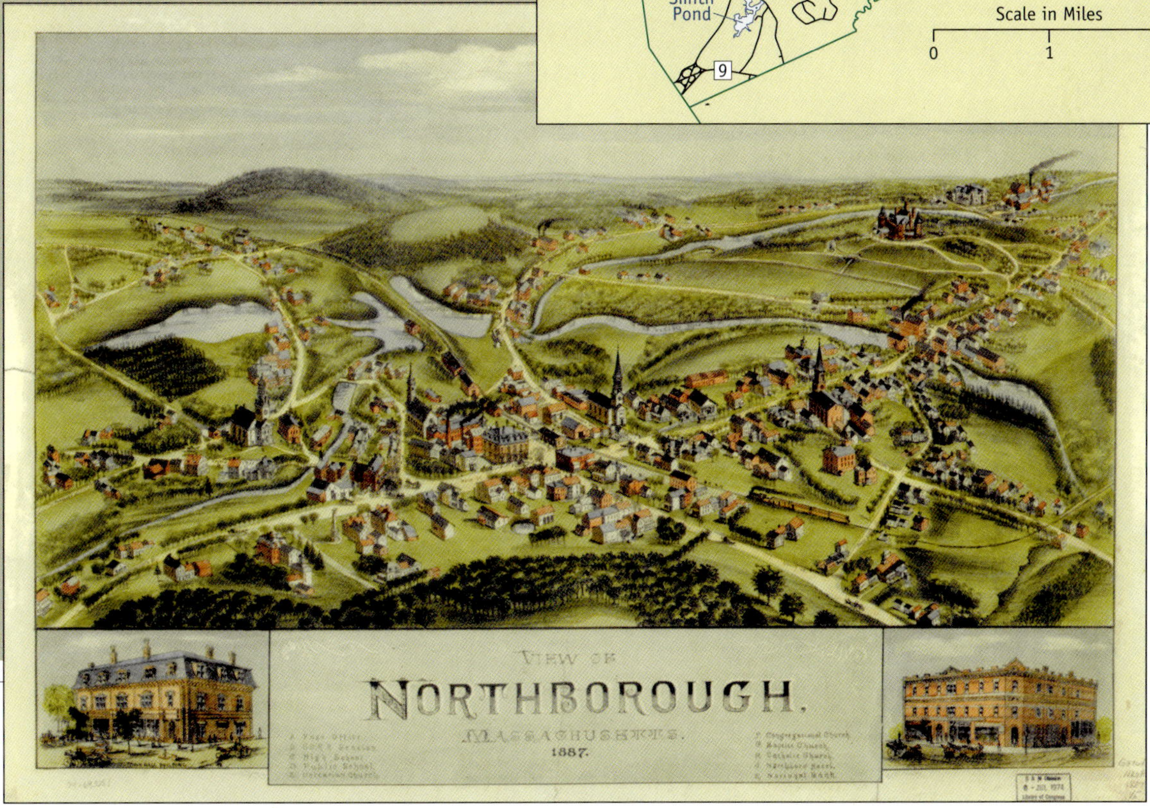

Lesson 1

Memory Master

1. What is a landmark?
2. List three ways your town has changed through time.

Lesson 2

Local Government

WORDS TO UNDERSTAND

citizen
income
influence
law
local government
order
public
volunteer

What Is Local Government?

Our country has a government. Our state also has a government. Did you know that your city or town also has a government?

City or town government is called ***local government.*** That means it is close to home. It helps the people in your town.

Why Do We Have Local Governments?

Different places have different needs. In some parts of our state, tall buildings are everywhere. The streets are crowded with cars and people. In other parts of our state, farms or beaches spread over the land. There are fewer people, and life is quiet. Local governments make rules and laws that fit the people in the community.

Activity

Everyday Rules

Whatever we do, wherever we go, we have to follow rules. If you get a new game for your birthday, you and your friends read the rules before you play. When you join a soccer team, the coach explains the rules.

Your family has rules, like "You can't stay up late on a school night," and "Don't throw your clothes on the floor." We learn many rules when we are very young. We hardly even think about them as we grow up.

List some rules under each heading below. It's fun to do this in groups.

Home Rules	Eating Rules	Town Rules
______	______	______
______	______	______
Classroom Rules	**Favorite Sport or Game Rules**	**Traveling Rules**
______	______	______
______	______	______

Two Important Jobs

Let's look at two of the most important things local governments do:

Provide Order

Pretend there are no traffic lights or stop signs, and three cars come to an intersection at the same time. If none of the cars stops, there will be an accident. How do we know whose turn it is to go through the intersection?

We know because we have rules. Rules tell us who has to stop and who gets to go. They make things run smoothly. They also make things safer.

People in a community agree to follow certain rules or ***laws.*** Local governments make laws to keep ***order.***

Protect Rights

As a ***citizen*** of your town, you have rights. Local governments protect your rights.

Let's say you park your new bike outside. While you are inside playing, someone steals your bike. You are mad because you know this is not fair. What can you do?

You can go to the police. They will try to find your bike. They will try to catch the person who stole it. The police and the local laws are there to protect your rights.

Here is another example. Just last week, "Heavy Metal" Williams moved in next door to you. He is in a band called Explosion. He plays the electric guitar, drums, and keyboard. The band likes to practice at Heavy Metal's home so they can be good enough to go on tour.

You need some peace and quiet so you can do your homework. Your baby sister needs to sleep. What can you do?

Cities and towns have laws about how much noise we can make. You could talk to Mr. Williams and explain how the noise is hurting your family. Maybe he will find another place to practice. If he does not, you can call the police and report him. If your town does not have a law about noise, you could go to the town meeting and talk about the problem. You could ask the town leaders to make a new law.

Boston has rules about how tall a building can be. What types of rules do you think small towns need?

Governments Provide Services

Local governments serve the people. They keep order and protect rights. They also provide services like these:

- *Public* schools
- Public parks, beaches, and swimming pools
- Police departments
- Fire departments
- Libraries
- Snow plows
- New roads and road repairs
- Garbage pick-up

How many public services can you find in this town?

SCHOOL
SCHOOL
POLICE
LIBRARY
HEALTH CARE
WATER

Taxes Pay for Services

How do local governments pay for the services they provide? They get money from taxes. A tax is money that people pay to the government.

Everybody has to give some of their money to the government. Taxes are a way of sharing the cost of things that we all want.

Sales Tax

When you buy a new toy at the store, you pay a sales tax. The sales tax in Massachusetts is five percent. That means that for every dollar you spend, you must pay an extra five cents that goes to the state government.

In our state, some goods do not have a sales tax. There is no sales tax on clothes, food, newspapers, or tickets to sporting events or amusement parks.

Income Tax

People and businesses pay taxes on the money they make. This is called an ***income*** tax. Your parents have to pay income tax every year.

Property Tax

If you own land, a home, or a building, you have to pay property tax.

Working Together

It takes many workers to provide government services. Some workers get paid for their work. Others are volunteers. A ***volunteer*** is someone who gives his or her time to help others without getting paid. Do you know anyone who volunteers at a hospital, library, or school?

People in Natick started a program called the Neighborhood Bus. At every hour, the bus starts at the town common and goes through the town. Many people are happy to use this service.

The Lowell Folk Festival takes place every summer. The city of Lowell and hundreds of volunteers work together to make it happen. At the festival you can see crafts, eat many different foods, watch folk dancing, and listen to music from many cultures.

Community Leaders

The people vote for leaders for their town. Cities and towns have a **mayor** or a **town manager**. The mayor runs the town with the help of a **council**. Sometimes the council is called a select board or selectmen.

The **police chief** is in charge of the police force. The **fire chief** is in charge of the fire department. The **superintendent** runs the public schools.

YOUR TOWN

Who are the leaders in your community? Most towns have a website on the Internet. Visit your town's website to find out about the leaders in your community. Make a poster showing their pictures. Under each picture write the person's name and what he or she does for your town.

The People Choose

The most important thing to remember about our government is that citizens get to choose who will lead their communities.

Most people who are citizens of the United States and are at least 18 years old can vote for their leaders.

Most towns in Massachusetts still have town meetings. In some towns, people choose representatives to speak for them at town meetings. If town leaders and representatives do not make laws the people want, the people can vote for different representatives at the next election.

You Can Make a Difference

People can make a difference in their communities. They can *influence* their local government. They can:

Go to town meetings

Vote

Run for office

When you grow up, you can do all of these things too. What can you do right now? There are many things you can do today to help your community and be a good citizen:

- Obey all of your family rules.
- Obey all of your school rules.
- Tell the truth.
- Be polite and helpful.
- Help keep your own home and yard clean.
- Never litter.
- Never ruin someone else's property.
- Ask adults in your family to vote.
- Write a letter to the editor of your town's newspaper. (Letters from kids often get printed!)
- Talk with adults about what is going on in your town.

What other things can you do? Make a list with your class.

Memory Master

Lesson 2

1. Name two important jobs that local governments do.
2. Give three examples of services from the local government.
3. Why do people have to pay taxes?
4. Name two types of taxes.
5. Give an example of a town or city leader.

Lesson 3

Local Economics

WORDS TO UNDERSTAND
barter
economics
specialization
trade

Economics in Your Community

People have needs. They need food, water, clothing, heat, shelter, and health care. People also have wants. They want things like cars, books, toys, and education.

How do people get the things they need and want? Today, they buy these things with money.

How do people get money? Most people work at jobs and get paid. Then they decide what they will buy with their money.

Goods and Services

Things that people make to sell are called goods. Bikes, video games, cell phones, cookies, milk, chairs, desks, and chalk are goods. Goods are made in factories, workshops, or even at home. Things people grow, like fruits and grains, are also goods.

People need medical care from doctors and nurses. They need education from teachers. They may need help fixing their washing machines or computers. Doctors, nurses, teachers, and repair people provide services. Services are things that people do for other people.

Economics is the study of how people get the goods and services they need and want. In most communities, there are people who make or sell the things that other people in the community need and want.

Activity

Goods or Services?

On a separate piece of paper, number from 1 to 12. Write "G" next to the jobs that produce goods. Write "S" next to the jobs that perform services.

1. Fixes the plumbing
2. Collects the garbage
3. Teaches students
4. Makes paint
5. Paints pictures to sell
6. Makes cars
7. Repairs cars
8. Delivers pizza
9. Makes telephones
10. Makes toys
11. Sells houses
12. ____________ (What you would like to do when you grow up)

Native Americans traded furs for English cloth.

Trade and Barter

People didn't always use money to pay for food, shoes, tools, and other things they needed. How did they pay for things?

The simplest way was to barter or ***trade*** with each other. For example, a farmer might trade extra eggs for shoes. The farmer would get new shoes. The shoemaker would get fresh eggs.

Bartering did not always work. For example, what if the shoemaker already had enough eggs? If the farmer could give him money, the shoemaker could buy something else. Can you see how money often made trading easier?

Barter is the exchange of goods and services without using money.

Activity

Making a Trade

Have you ever traded baseball cards with your friends? Have you traded your cookie for your friend's brownie? Think of a trade you have made. What did you give up? What did you get? Do you think it was a fair trade? Write about your experience with trading. Use complete sentences. Then choose a friend and role-play a trade you would like to make.

Specialization

The farmer and the shoemaker had different skills. The farmer knew how to plant and tend a field. He had the time to water the crops. He knew when to pick them. The shoemaker knew how to cut and sew leather. He was good at making shoes. Someone else in the village was good at making candles. She made candles all day and sold them to others.

Specialization is when people produce only one kind of product or are skilled at one job. The workers become very skilled, but they have to count on others to do the rest.

People and companies are more specialized today than they were in the past. For example, today there are many different kinds of farmers. Some are dairy farmers. Some only grow corn. Others grow tobacco or cranberries. These are examples of specialization.

Look at this picture of the different jobs in a bicycle factory. Start at number one. Then find number two, and so on. Can you see why it would be hard for one worker to do all the jobs?

Memory Master

Lesson 3

1. What is economics?
2. Give two examples of goods.
3. Give two examples of services.
4. What is barter?
5. What is specialization? Give an example.

The Many Jobs in a BIKE FACTORY

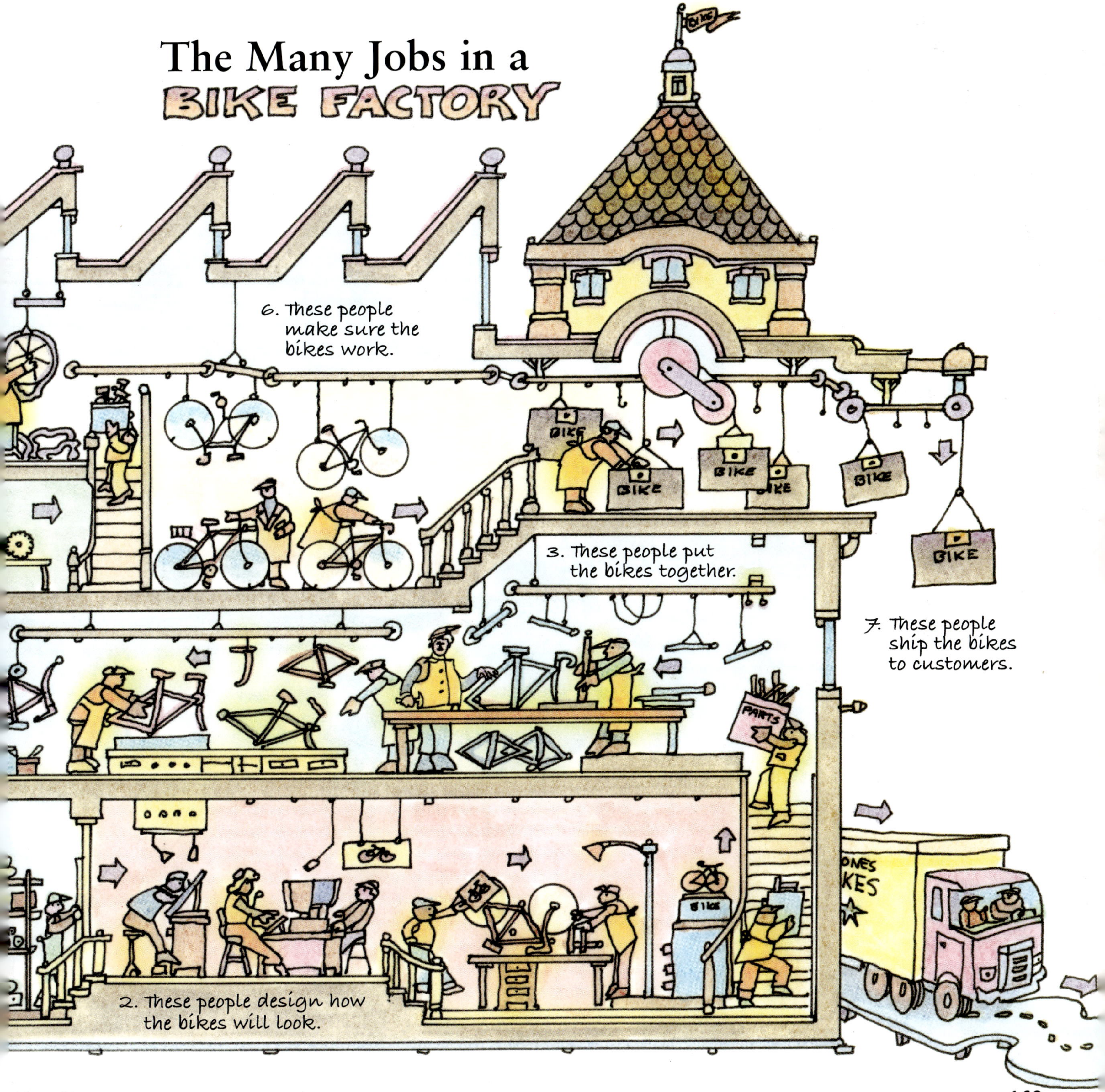

Chapter 7 Review

What's the Point?

Each town has its own history. You can learn about your town's past at a museum or historical society. Old maps and pictures can teach you about the past. You can also learn by asking the people around you how your town has changed over time.

Different towns have different needs. We have local governments to meet the people's needs. Local governments provide order, protect rights, and offer services. The people pay for these services through taxes.

How do the people in your town make a living? This is part of economics. Different places have different stores and businesses. People specialize in certain goods or services.

Activity

Make a Map of Your Community

Follow these steps to make a map of your town or neighborhood. Do your first draft in pencil. You might need to erase a few times to get it right!

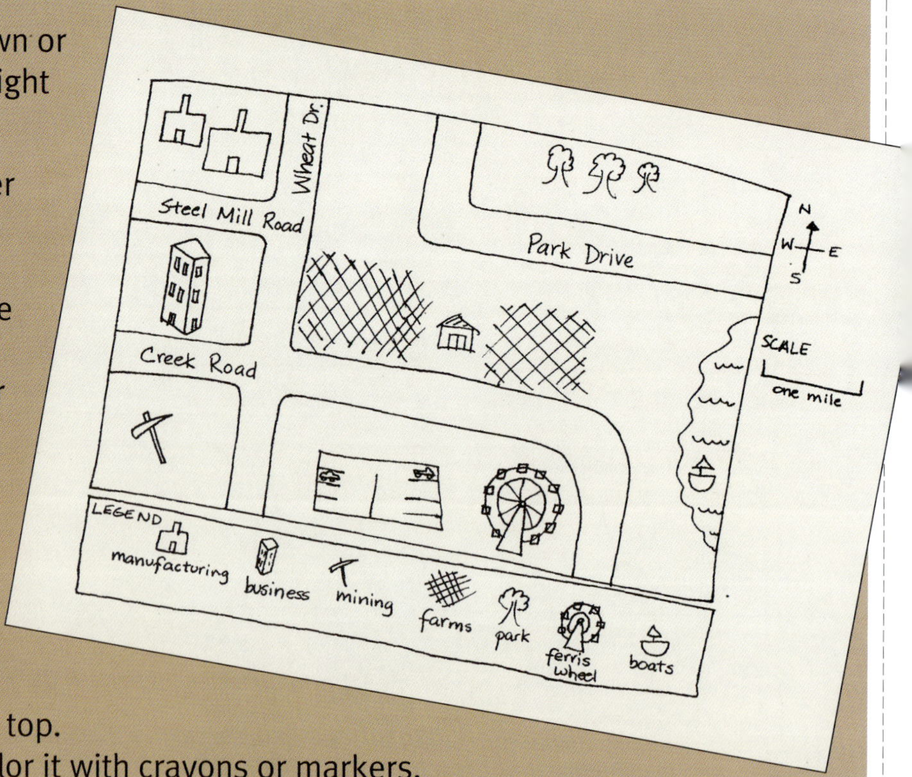

1. Draw the main streets. You can use another map for help.
2. Add symbols for your house, your friend's house, your school, the post office, and the police or fire department.
3. Add any landmarks or historic sites to your map.
4. Make a key to show what the symbols stand for.
5. Draw a compass to show north, south, east, and west. Use the cardinal directions to help you place things on the map.
6. Think of a title for your map. Write it at the top.
7. When your map is just how you want it, color it with crayons or markers.

Activity

People of Your Community

What different groups of people have settled in your community since it was founded?

1. Find out if any new groups came in the 1700s, 1800s, and 1900s. Find out who came in the 21st century.
2. On a wall map of the world, mark your town with a tack.
3. Now mark all the countries from which these people came.
4. Use four different colors of yarn. Choose one color to stand for each century. For example, blue could be for the 1700s, red for the 1800s, and so on.
5. Use the yarn to connect the countries to your town. The colors should show when people came from each country. For example, if people came from England in the 1700s, use blue yarn to connect England to your town.
6. Make a key to go with your map.
7. Vote for a title for your map.

Activity

Workers in Your Community

What goods and services are sold in your community? Visit a busy street in your town, or look in the yellow pages of the phone book. What businesses do you see there? What kinds of things do people do for a living? Make one list of the goods you find. Make another list of the services you find.

Goods	Services

People in Our Past

Have you ever heard of Louisa May Alcott? She was a writer from Concord. She lived in the 19th century.

Louisa May Alcott started writing to make money. She wanted to do something to help support her family. She wrote a book called Little Women. *It became famous.*

Today, you can visit the Alcott House in Concord. In this picture, a woman dressed as Louisa May Alcott shows children a game.

Louisa May Alcott is one person from Massachusetts who made history. In this chapter you will learn about some other famous people from our state.

Chapter 8

"Far away there in the sunshine are my highest [hopes]. I may not reach them, but I can look up and see their beauty, believe in them, and try to follow where they lead."

—Louisa May Alcott

Photo ©Kindra Clineff

Lesson 1

Famous People

PEOPLE TO KNOW
Susan B. Anthony
Clara Barton
Alexander Graham Bell
Emily Dickinson
W.E.B. Du Bois
Robert Goddard
John F. Kennedy
Francis Cabot Lowell
Henry David Thoreau
An Wang

WORDS TO UNDERSTAND
civil rights
encourage
industrial
liquid
lynch
manufacturing
patent
prejudice
recluse
scholarship
self-reliance
solid
suffrage

People We Remember

People from Massachusetts have done great things. Some worked quietly by themselves. They painted pictures or wrote poems. Some made speeches in front of a crowd. Others invented things or helped others. Each one made history. Let's read about some of the people from our state who are famous today.

Clara Barton

1821–1912

Clara Barton was from Oxford. She was born on Christmas Day in 1821. Her full name was Clarissa Harlowe Barton.

Clara was the youngest of five children. Her brothers and sisters taught her to read and do math. They also taught her to ride horses. She loved animals and had two horses and a dog.

When Clara was eight years old, she went away to boarding school. She missed her family very much. Her father brought her back to Oxford.

Clara grew up and became a teacher. She started her own school in North Oxford.

The First Woman at the Patent Office

After teaching school for many years, Clara went to work in the U.S. Patent Office. That is where the government gives ***patents*** to people who invent things. A patent says who the inventor was. Clara was the first woman to work there.

"Angel of the Battlefield"

Before long, our country was at war. The states in the North fought the states in the South. It was called the Civil War.

Clara wanted to help. She became a nurse. She was working in Washington, D.C., when some soldiers from Massachusetts stopped there. They had lost their supplies. Clara cooked for them and tore up sheets to make bandages. She brought the soldiers food, clothing, and other supplies. She took care of the men in army camps and on the battlefield.

People started calling Clara the "Angel of the Battlefield." She won medals for her work.

The Red Cross

After the war, Clara went to Europe. She learned about the Red Cross. It was a group of people who helped others in wartime. They brought food and water to people who had none. They helped the sick. They taught people how to be healthy.

Clara wanted to start the Red Cross in America. She told the president it was a good idea for our country to join this group. He agreed, and Clara was made the first president of the American Red Cross. She had that job for 25 years.

We remember Clara Barton because she helped so many people. She made a difference in their lives.

What do you think?

Clara Barton made a decision to help in the war. Have you made a decision in your life to do something hard? Did it change things in your life?

The Arts

Henry David Thoreau

1817–1862

Trees, rivers, rocks, animals, a pond, a small garden, a good book—these things were everything to Henry David Thoreau. He was a writer, thinker, and lover of nature. He thought people would be happier living simple lives close to nature.

A Young Boy in Concord

Henry David Thoreau was born in Boston. When he was still a young boy, his family moved to Concord. His father made pencils for a living.

Henry loved Concord. He played in the woods and explored the pond nearby. He liked to take long walks. As he walked, he looked and listened. He liked to think as he walked in the woods.

Henry was the only one of the four children in his family to go to college. He went to Harvard. He became a teacher, but he soon quit. He did not want to whip his students when they did not behave. In those days, that was the way teachers punished their students. He tried teaching again with his brother John. They started a school together, but John got very sick and died. Henry was too sad to go on with the school alone.

In Good Company

Thoreau had a group of friends who liked to think and write. One of his friends was named Ralph Waldo Emerson. Emerson was older and taught him many things. He taught him to keep a journal. Thoreau wrote down the things he thought about for the rest of his life. He used his journal to help him write about nature and people. Thoreau was also a friend of another writer named Nathaniel Hawthorne.

"I Went to the Woods . . ."

To live out his ideas, Thoreau built a small cabin next to Walden Pond. He lived there for two years. He worked in his garden and read books. He fished and wrote in his journal. Every day he spent time enjoying nature. He studied plants, animals, and the weather.

Although he liked to be alone, every few days he went to the village. He visited friends and heard the latest news. Sometimes he had friends over. He talked to woodsmen who came to the forest.

Some of Thoreau's best writings came from the time he spent at Walden Pond. His most famous book is called *Walden*. Thoreau had a good sense of humor. He wrote about changing the week to six days of rest and one day of work. It wasn't all a joke—he wanted people to see that they did not need to rush around busy all the time. They could make or grow what they needed to live. They could do things for themselves. This is called ***self-reliance.***

What do you think?

Are there any "extra" things in your life that you could do without? What are they? What would your life be like without them?

Photo ©Kindra Clineff

One Can Make a Difference

After living at the pond, Thoreau kept writing and doing important things. He loved freedom, so he hated slavery. He and his family helped runaway slaves escape to freedom. He wrote about a time when he spent a night in jail for standing up to a law he thought was wrong. He tried to show that one person can make a difference.

Thoreau died in Concord when he was only 44 years old. He was buried near many of his friends on Author's Ridge in Sleepy Hollow Cemetery.

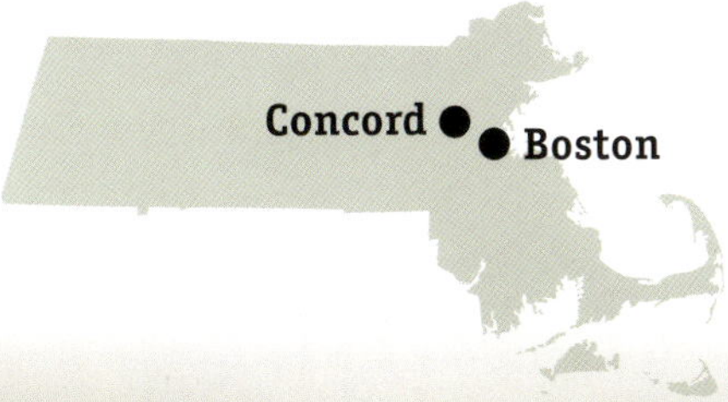

Henry David Thoreau also wrote about hiking along the Concord and Merrimack Rivers.

"In warm evenings I . . . sat in the boat playing the flute, and saw the perch [fish], which I seemed to have charmed, hovering around me, and the moon traveling over the ribbed bottom, which was strewed with the wrecks of the forest."

—from *Walden*,
by Henry David Thoreau

The Arts

Emily Dickinson

1830–1886

Emily Dickinson was a poet. Maybe you have read her poem about a snake, or one about a bird, cat, or bee. She also wrote about big subjects like nature, life, and death. For the most part, she wrote her poems in secret. She was not famous until after she died.

This picture was taken when Emily Dickinson was a teenager. Many years later, in a letter to a friend, she described what she looked like. She said she was small, her hair was like a chestnut burr, and her eyes were the color of sherry that a guest might leave behind.

Courtesy of the Amherst College Archives and Special Collections

An Amherst Girl

Emily was born in Amherst. She lived there all of her life. Her parents and grandparents were very involved in education. Emily learned a lot as a child.

Emily was bright and funny. She loved books. She also loved nature. She liked to watch the seasons change, and she noticed everything. She grew flowers in her garden. When the weather turned cold, she grew flowers in a greenhouse her father built for her.

A Quiet Life

As Emily Dickinson grew older, she stayed at home and saw only her closest friends. People called her a ***recluse.*** That means she wanted to be by herself and not with people she didn't know well.

At home, Dickinson led a busy life. She did the baking for the family. Everyone loved her gingerbread. She tended her flowers. She took walks with her dog Carlo. She wrote many letters to friends and loved ones. Most of all, she liked to write poems and think about things.

Sometimes while she was baking or doing chores, she got an idea for a poem. She scribbled the idea down on a scrap of paper like a recipe, an envelope, or even the back of a chocolate wrapper. Later, when she had more time, she made it into a poem.

At night in her room, she copied some of her poems onto paper and sewed them together with string. She kept the booklets in her drawer. Sometimes she put poems in letters to her friends. She wrote almost 1,800 poems in her life.

A Remarkable Discovery

When Emily died, her sister found her poems. She wanted to get them published so more people could read them. It took a few years to get them ready. When the first book of Emily's poems came out, people liked them. Over time, more and more people read them. Today, she is one of the most famous poets in America.

You can take a tour of Emily Dickinson's home in Amherst.
You can see her bedroom, where she wrote most of her poems.

I'm Nobody! Who are you?
Are you–Nobody–too?
Then there's a pair of us!
Dont tell! they'd advertise–you know!

How dreary–to be–Somebody!
How public–like a Frog–
To tell one's name–the livelong June–
To an admiring Bog!

—Emily Dickinson

Francis Cabot Lowell

1775–1817

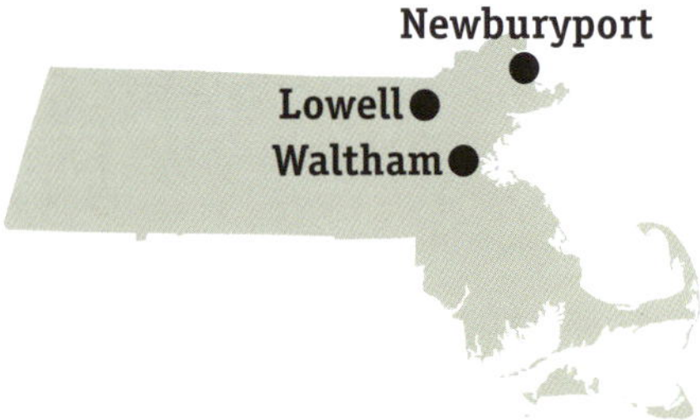

An Important Trip

Francis Cabot Lowell was born in Newburyport. His father was a judge and one of America's richest lawyers. The family moved to Boston when Francis was still young.

Lowell was interested in making textiles. These are fabrics made by knitting or weaving. American women used spinning wheels and looms. They made cloth for their families. What if a machine could do these jobs?

Lowell heard about textile machines in Europe. He went to England and Scotland to learn about them. He saw factories with looms that could weave hundreds of yards of fabric each day.

Building on an Idea

When Francis Lowell came back home, he worked out a plan. He said all the steps needed to turn raw cotton into cloth could be done in one factory. He started the Boston Manufacturing Company. ***Manufacturing*** means making something with machines.

Lowell built the first power loom in America. It was even better than the ones he had seen in England. He built a factory in Waltham on the Charles River. It used the river for power. It was the first factory in America to make textiles all under one roof. It opened in 1814 and was a big success.

Lowell, Massachusetts

Lowell and his partners wanted to build factories in other towns. They planned a town on the Merrimack and Concord Rivers.

When Lowell died, his partners kept going with the plan. The men built mills and homes for workers and their families. They built stores and churches. The company owned everything in the town. They hired young women to work in the mills. They named the town Lowell.

Lowell became one of America's first ***industrial*** cities. Other mills and factories were built along the Merrimack River.

The new textile mills were one of the first places to hire women to do most of the work. This was also one of the first times that women were paid for their work.

At first, the company tried to make life good for the workers. The girls lived in apartments next to the factory. Bells rang for getting up, starting work, eating meals, and going to bed. All of the workers had to go to one of the churches on Sunday.

The mill girls took pride in their work. They published their own writings in a magazine called the Lowell Offering.

An Wang

1920–1990

"Progress does not follow a straight line."
—Dr. An Wang

An Wang always thought people should give more to their community than they got. His ideas helped bring about today's computer. He was also one of the first to create a desktop calculator.

From China to Boston

An Wang was born in Shanghai, China. Find that city on a map in your classroom. It is a long way from Massachusetts.

An Wang was the oldest of five children. His father started teaching him English when he was four years old. An Wang went to college when he was only 16.

An Wang lived through very hard times in China. Both of his parents and one sister died because of wars in his country. An Wang studied hard so he could have a better life. He worked for a science magazine. He went to college. Later, he taught electrical engineering.

In 1945, An Wang came to the United States. He got a Ph.D. from Harvard. A Ph.D. is the highest degree a person can get. He started his own business in Boston. He called it Wang Laboratories, Inc. Later, the company moved to Tewksbury.

Computers and Memory

An Wang invented a way to store information on a small metal ring. It was an early way to store memory in a computer. Years later, the microchip replaced the ring. Sometimes people called An Wang "Data Bank" or the "Doctor" because his work helped science in so many ways. (A data bank is a place where lots of information is stored.)

Giving to Others

An Wang was a very quiet man. He gave a lot of money to help science. He also loved art. He gave money to help artists in Boston. The Wang Center for Performing Arts is named after him.

Alexander Graham Bell

1847–1922

The next time you hear a telephone ring, think about Alexander Graham Bell. He invented the telephone in 1876. He also had other great ideas that helped shape our world.

A Curious Boy

Alexander Bell was born in Scotland. Later his family moved to Boston. They called him Aleck. His mother was almost deaf, but she could play the piano. She taught him to play the piano. She also taught him the alphabet used by deaf people.

Everyone in the Bell family thought sounds and voices were interesting. Alexander's grandfather was an expert on how people speak. His father studied speech problems. He ***encouraged*** Aleck and Aleck's brother to study speech. He said they should try and make a speaking machine. The boys used their barking dog for one experiment.

Alexander loved to read about science. He made his first invention when he was only 11. It was a tool to take wheat out of its husk.

Working With the Deaf

Bell became a professor at Boston University. He taught deaf people to speak. He met a young deaf woman named Mabel Hubbard. They fell in love and, after a few years, were married.

The First Telephone

Bell wanted to see if voices could be sent over a wire. He made a machine that would do this.

To test it, he stood in a room holding one end of the machine. His assistant, Thomas Watson, stood in the next room holding the other end. Then Alexander said the first words ever sent across a telephone wire: "Mr. Watson—come here—I want to see you."

The new machine was called a telephone. Bell and Watson took it to the World's Fair in Philadelphia. They showed the people what the phone could do. Everyone was amazed. Soon the Bell Telephone Company was started.

Other Dreams

Alexander Bell made a lot of money from his invention. He used some of the money to help others. He paid for a school to teach deaf students. He started the National Geographic Society and its magazine.

The inventor still had other dreams. He worked with kites and early models for airplanes. He blew fans across large blocks of ice to make an air conditioner. He invented the fastest watercraft in the world. It was a boat that skimmed over the water at 71 miles per hour.

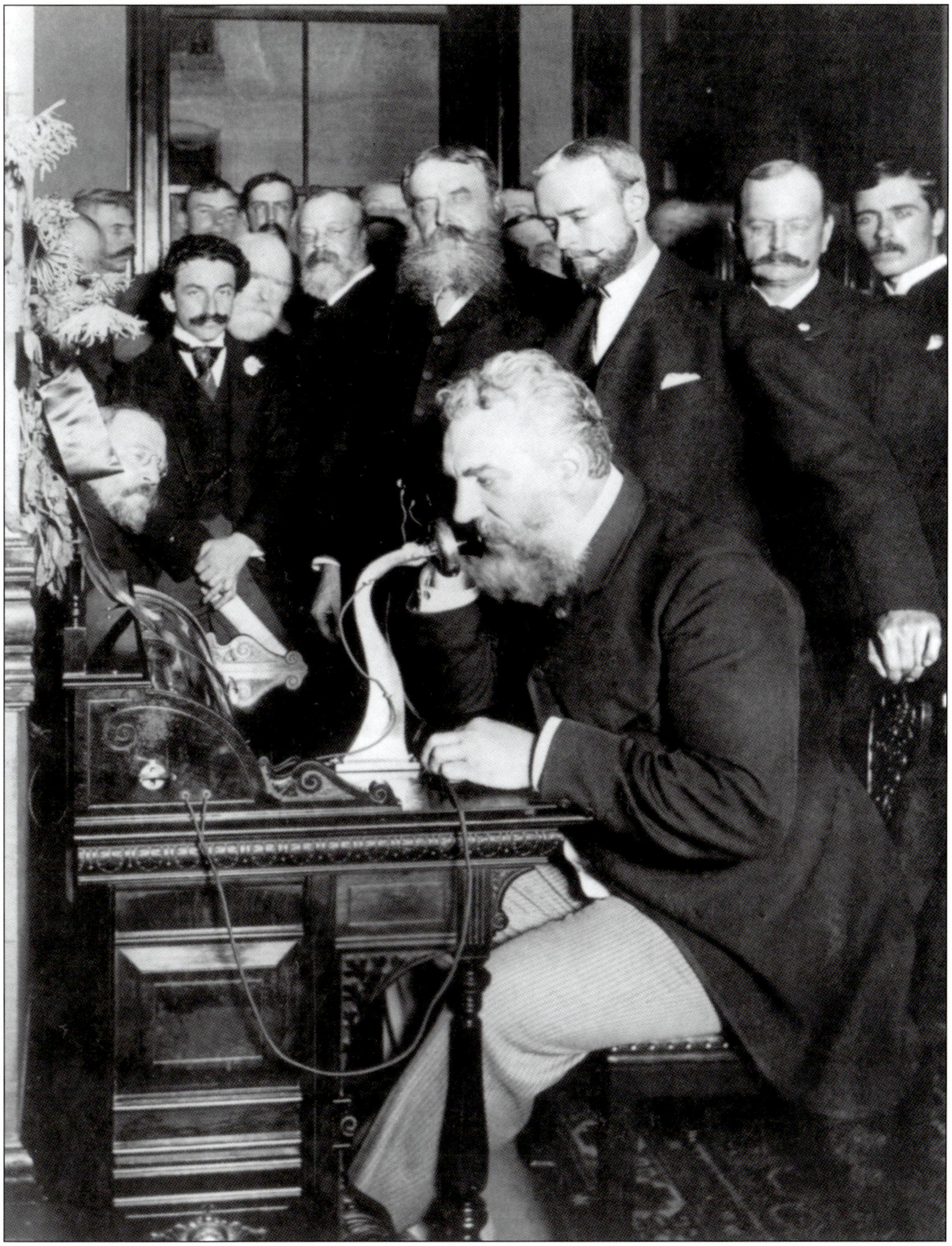

Alexander Graham Bell showed how his telephone worked. How is his telephone different from phones today?

What do you think?

Alexander Graham Bell once said,

"Leave the beaten track . . . and dive into the woods. Every time you do so you will . . . find something that you have never seen before. Follow it up, explore all around it, and before you know it, you will have something worth thinking about."

What do you think he meant by leaving the track and diving into the woods? Do you think he meant we should really go out in the woods, or do you think the woods stand for something else? What might they stand for?

Robert H. Goddard

1882–1945

Science

Robert Goddard called October 19th "Anniversary Day." It was the day of his first dream in the cherry tree.

A Boy and a Dream

Young Robert Goddard dreamed of sending something so high it could reach Mars. When he was 17, he climbed an old cherry tree in his yard in Worcester. He was supposed to be cutting off its dead branches. Instead he started daydreaming.

He looked up into the sky. He thought about what kind of machine might be able to travel so far away. In those days, people still traveled by wagon, train, or steamship. They laughed at the idea of flying machines, but Robert wanted to follow his dream.

The young man went to college. He studied math and science. He became a professor and studied rockets. He worked hard on his ideas. People called him "Moon Man," but he did not give up.

A Big Idea

Dr. Goddard knew the BANG of fireworks came from ***solid*** fuel. He wanted to see if ***liquid*** fuels would make a rocket go farther than the quick blast of fireworks.

In Auburn, the inventor tested the first rocket that used liquid fuel. It went only 41 feet, but his idea had worked! For many more years, he worked on his rockets. He made some that went 500 miles an hour and over 2,000 feet in the air.

Going Down in History

The government did not pay much attention to Goddard's work until after he died. Today, he is known as the father of modern rockets. The Goddard Space Flight Center near Washington, D.C., is named after him.

What do you think?

What if Robert Goddard had given up when people called him names? How might the world be different today?

Susan B. Anthony

1820–1906

Politics

Susan Brownell Anthony worked hard for women's rights. She led the struggle to help women win the right to vote. She spent much of her life trying to bring about change.

"It was we the people; not we, the white male citizens; nor yet we, the male citizens; but we, the whole people, who formed the Union."
—Susan B. Anthony

A Girl From Adams

Susan was born in Adams. She was one of eight children. Their father taught them to believe in themselves, work hard, and stand up for what they knew was right.

Susan learned to read and write when she was only three. Her family moved to New York when she was six. Susan started school there. The teacher would not show her how to do long division. He said it was for boys. When her father heard this, he took Susan out of school. He set up a home school and hired a woman to teach her.

Later, Susan became a teacher. She had a problem with her eyes, but she did not let that stop her. After an operation, she could see just fine, but her right eye always turned out a little. She did not like the way it looked. Sometimes when her picture was taken, she only showed her left side.

Working for Change

Susan B. Anthony worked for change in many ways. She wanted people to stop drinking alcohol. She wanted to get rid of slavery. She worked to free the slaves before the Civil War.

In those days, women had fewer rights than they do now. They were not allowed to vote. If they were married, they could not own property. Many men did not think of them as equals. Susan and some of her friends started a women's group. They spoke out about these things. They talked about getting women the same rights as men.

Susan B. Anthony made women's rights her main goal. She and her friend Elizabeth Cady Stanton started the National Woman's Suffrage Association. *Suffrage* means the right to vote. Anthony was president of the group.

The group talked to people everywhere about women's rights. They tried to change the laws. They tried to help people see that women should be able to vote.

One time, Susan B. Anthony voted for a president even though women were not allowed to vote. She was arrested and had to pay a $100 fine. She told the court she would never pay the fine. She never did.

Never Give Up

Until the end of her life, Susan B. Anthony spoke out for women's rights. The law that gave women the right to vote came only after her death.

Many years later, the government wanted to honor Susan B. Anthony. They created a one-dollar coin with her picture on it.

W.E.B. Du Bois

1868–1963

Politics

"One could not be a calm, cool, . . . scientist while Negroes were lynched, murdered, and starved."

—W.E.B. Du Bois

W.E.B. Du Bois was born in a time when most black people and white people lived separate lives. They lived in separate parts of the cities. They went to separate schools. They ate at separate lunch counters and sat in different parts of theaters. Many white people did not want to believe that black people were equal to them.

Du Bois thought black people should have every chance, or opportunity, that white people had. He spent his long life working to make things better for African Americans.

Going South

Du Bois was born in Great Barrington. His father left the family, so W.E.B. lived with his mother. There were not many African Americans in Great Barrington. Both white and black children went to the same school.

Du Bois wanted to go to Harvard. He was smart enough, but he did not have the money. He got a ***scholarship*** to Fisk University in Tennessee. His family and friends also helped him to pay for school.

Things were much different in Tennessee than they were in Massachusetts. Du Bois saw how poorly black people were treated. Those who tried to make things better were hanged, or ***lynched.*** Du Bois studied how the people lived and worked together. This kind of work is called social science. He was one of the first African Americans to do this kind of work.

A Harvard Ph.D.

Du Bois graduated from Fisk, but he still wanted to go to Harvard. Finally, he made it. He studied there and became the first black person to get a Ph.D. from Harvard.

People were interested in the work Du Bois was doing. He went to Germany to study and teach. Then he taught in Ohio. He went to Philadelphia to study black neighborhoods.

The Souls of Black Folk

Du Bois wrote a book about being black in America. It was called *The Souls of Black Folk*. He wrote about the struggles black people faced:

> *"[The black person] simply wishes to make it possible . . . to be both a Negro and an American, without being cursed and spit upon by his fellows, without having the doors of Opportunity closed roughly in his face."*

Working for Equality

Du Bois worked with another black leader from Massachusetts named William Trotter. They formed a group to work for the rights of African Americans.

Soon after, Du Bois helped to start a new group called the National Association for the Advancement of Colored People (NAACP). Black people and white people worked together in this group. They wanted to end lynching and bring people together. Du Bois wrote for their magazine. He ended up leaving the NAACP, but the group is still at work today.

During World War I, black soldiers fought for our country. When they got home, they were still treated badly. Du Bois worked to get them fair treatment. Women also wanted fair treatment. They wanted to be able to vote. Du Bois supported their right to vote.

Going to Africa

Du Bois became interested in Africa. He started a meeting of African leaders called the Pan-African Congress. He decided to leave the United States and move to Africa. He lived and worked in Ghana until he died.

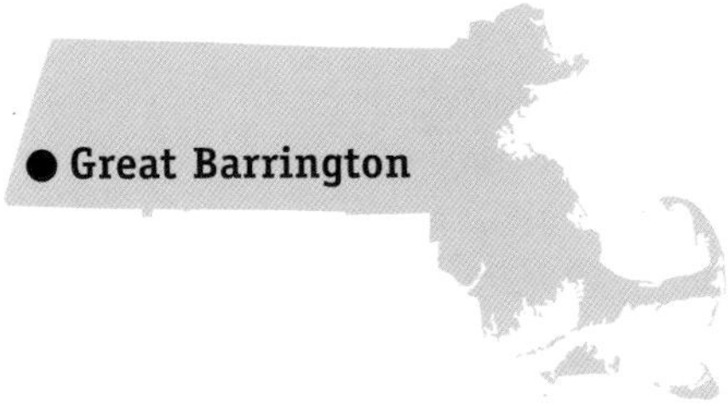

W.E.B. stands for William Edward Burghardt.

Politics

John F. Kennedy

1917–1963

You have probably heard of JFK. These letters stand for John Fitzgerald Kennedy. He was the youngest man ever elected president of the United States.

All in the Family

John Fitzgerald Kennedy was born in Brookline. His parents called him Jack.

Jack came from a family of politicians. His grandfathers had come from Ireland. When they came to America, there was a lot of ***prejudice*** against Irish Catholics. Prejudice is making judgments about people because of their race or religion. This only made Jack's relatives work harder. Both of his grandfathers went into politics. One became the mayor of Boston. Young Jack listened to this grandfather practice his speeches.

Jack's father also went into politics. He worked for our government in England. He took good care of Jack and his eight other children.

School Days

Jack was not an "A" student, but people liked him. He was very thin and often sick, but he loved sports. He played football and golf. He was a swimmer, and he won a trophy for sailing.

The Kennedy family had a house in Hyannis Port on Cape Cod. During the summer, they went there and had lots of fun. They swam, sailed, and played touch football.

Jack went to college at Harvard. He wrote for the school newspaper. His older brother Joe wanted to go into politics. Joe said he would be the first Catholic president.

One summer, Jack went to visit his father in England. World War II was going on, and Jack wrote a paper about it for school. Later, his paper was published as a book called *Why England Slept*.

War Stories

After college, Jack and Joe joined the navy. Jack was in charge of a boat. A Japanese torpedo hit his boat. It hurt his back very badly, but Jack saved the lives of three of his crew. He was given many medals for his bravery.

When Jack went home to Massachusetts, he learned some sad news. His brother Joe had died in the war. Jack wanted to make his family proud. He decided to run for Congress. He was elected to the House of Representatives, then to the Senate. He was on his way to becoming a great leader. If Joe couldn't be the first Catholic president, maybe Jack could.

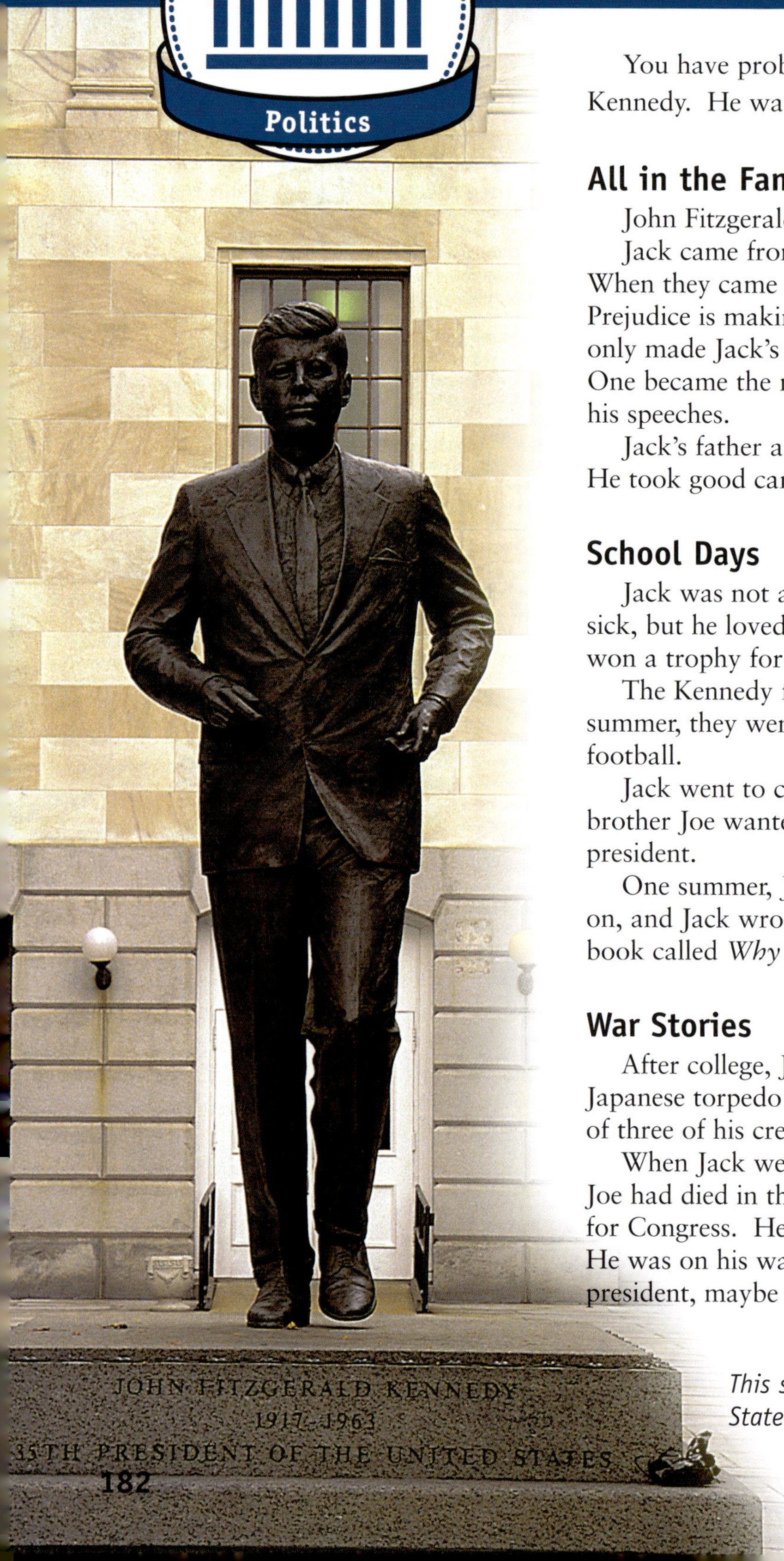

This statue is in front of the State House in Boston.

"Ask not what your country can do for you —ask what you can do for your country."
—John F. Kennedy

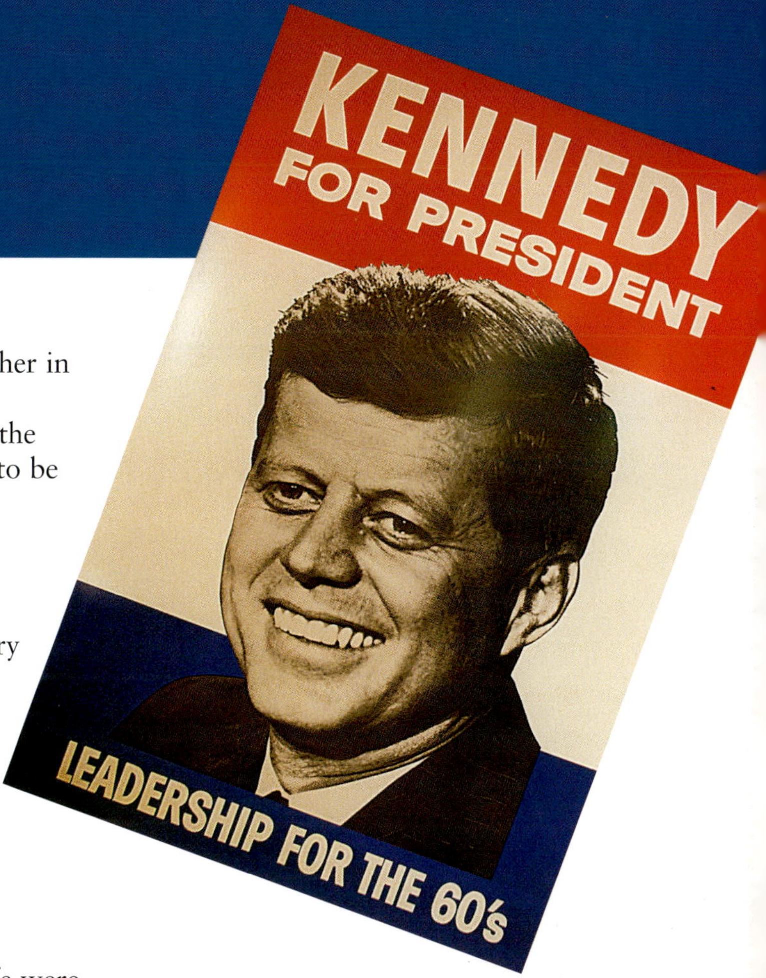

The Youngest President Ever Elected

Kennedy married Jacqueline Bouvier. She was a newspaper photographer in Washington. They had two children, Caroline and John Junior.

When John F. Kennedy was only 43 years old, he became president of the United States. The race was very close. Jack was the youngest man ever to be elected president. He was also the first Catholic president.

It was the 1960s, and television was still new. President Kennedy was handsome, confident, and intelligent. He used television to talk to the people. He went on television to talk about ***civil rights.*** He started the Peace Corps to help people around the world. He also wanted our country to lead the race to explore space.

The Kennedys made the White House a more interesting place. They invited lots of different people to visit. Mrs. Kennedy gave the rooms a makeover. She had a pre-school, swimming pool, and tree house built for the children. Even though Jack was a busy man, he always took time to play with his children.

Tragedy in Texas

In 1963, President Kennedy was visiting Dallas, Texas. He and his wife were riding in the back of a car when he was shot. He died a short time later.

People across the country were shocked and sad. Today, if you ask anyone over 45 years old about it, they will probably remember just what they were doing when they heard the news.

What do you think?

If you could sit down and talk to President Kennedy, what would you say to him? What questions would you ask him?

President Kennedy's brother Edward is one of our senators today.

Memory Master

Lesson 1

1. Name two inventors from Massachusetts. What did they invent?
2. Emily Dickinson was from the town of __________.
3. Susan B. Anthony worked for women's right to __________.
4. W.E.B. Du Bois wrote a book called ______________________________.
5. The youngest president elected in our country's history was ____________.

Chapter 8 Review

What's the Point?

People are the ones who make history. We remember famous people because they did something—maybe big, maybe small—that changed who we are. They may have made mistakes, but they kept trying.

Activity

Make an Illustrated Biography

1. Read a Biography

Many people from Massachusetts grew up to do important things. You can learn about more people by reading their biographies. Follow the steps below to read and make your own biography.

a) Choose a person from the list below, or think of another famous person from Massachusetts.

b) Use the library and Internet to read about the person's life. As you read, look for the answers to these questions:

- When was the person born?
- What century was it?
- What town or city did he or she come from? Locate it on a map.
- What kind of place was it when he or she lived there?
- What did the person do to make history?
- What things happened in the person's life that led to that?

SCIENCE AND TECHNOLOGY	THE ARTS	BUSINESS	EDUCATION, JOURNALISM, HEALTH	POLITICS
Alexander Graham Bell	Henry Adams	William Filene	Clara Barton	John Adams
Nathaniel Bowditch	Louisa May Alcott	Amos Lawrence	Dorothea Dix	John Quincy Adams
Robert Goddard	Leonard Bernstein	Francis Cabot Lowell	W.E.B Du Bois	Susan B. Anthony
John Hayes Hammond	John Singleton Copley	An Wang	Mary Lyon	Edward Brooke
Edwin Land	Emily Dickinson		Horace Mann	George H. Bush
Samuel Morse	Ralph Waldo Emerson		William Monroe Trotter	Calvin Coolidge
	Robert Frost			Benjamin Franklin
	Theodor Geisel			William Lloyd Garrison
	Nathaniel Hawthorne			Lewis Hayden
	Oliver Wendell Holmes			John F. Kennedy
	Frederick Law Olmsted			Paul Revere
	Norman Rockwell			
	Henry David Thoreau			

2. Make a Biography
Make a list of the big events in the person's life. Draw a picture for each event. Below the picture, write what happened. Put all the pictures in order on a poster to make a colorful biography.

3. What If?
Pick one event in the person's life. Think about what might have happened if that event had not occurred, or if it happened differently. Write a few paragraphs telling how you think the person's life would have been different and how history might have been different.

4. Missing Pieces
We don't know everything about everyone from the past. Often, there are pieces of the story that no one knows. Think about the person you chose. What DON'T you know about his or her life?

This activity is based on ideas from Myra Zarnowski's *History Makers: A Questioning Approach to Reading and Writing Biographies.*

New England, Physical Map

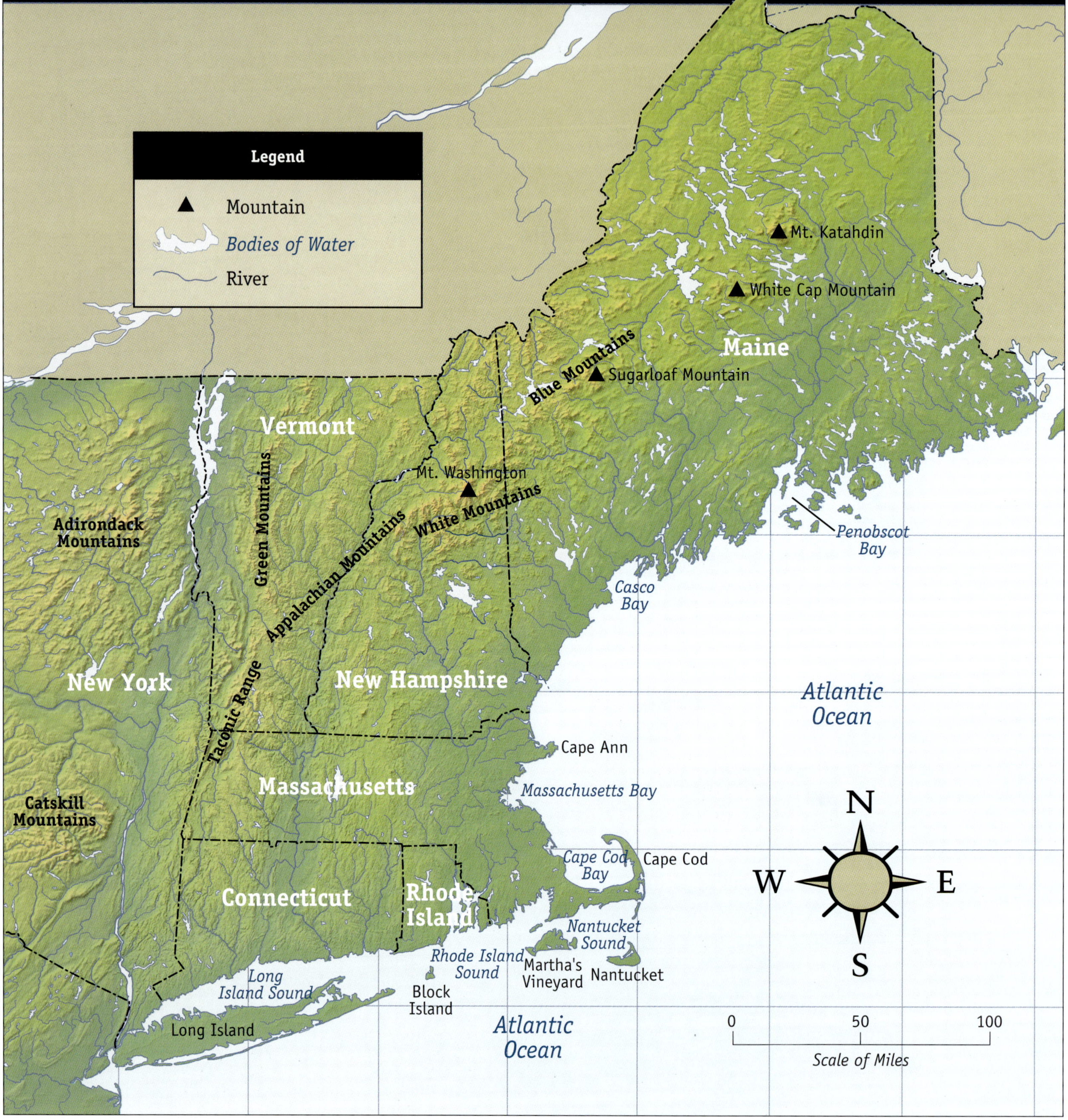

New England, Political Map
Legend
State Capital
International Border
State Border
CANADA
Maine
Vermont
New Hampshire
New York
Massachusetts
Connecticut
Rhode Island
Montpelier
Augusta
Concord
Albany
Boston
Hartford
Providence
Penobscot Bay
Casco Bay
Atlantic Ocean
Cape Anne
Massachusetts Bay
Cape Cod Bay
Cape Cod
Nantucket Sound
Nantucket
Martha's Vineyard
Rhode Island Sound
Block Island
Long Island Sound
Long Island
Atlantic Ocean
N
S
W
E
0
50
100
Scale of Miles

Massachusetts, Physical Map

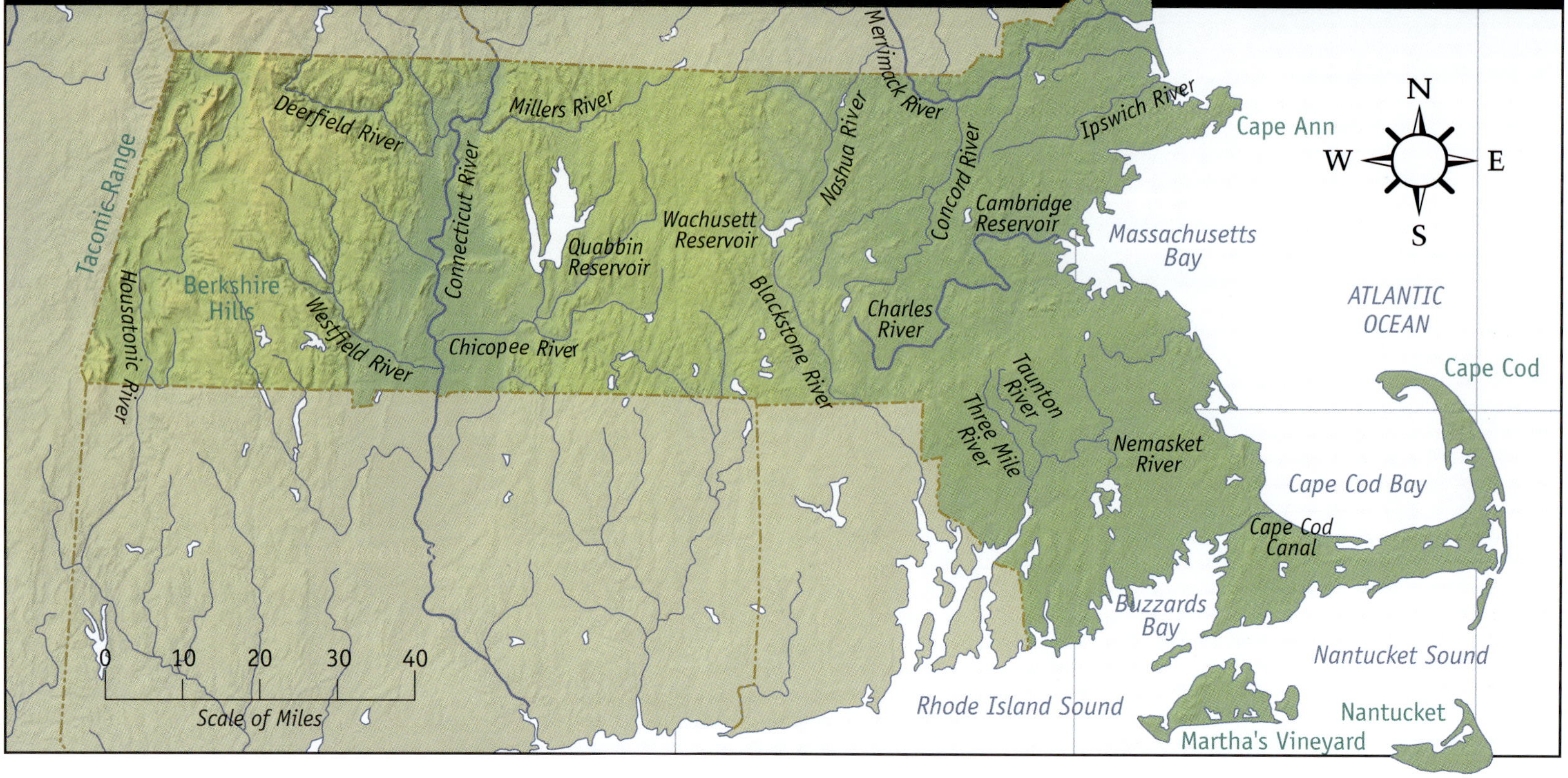

Massachusetts, Political Map

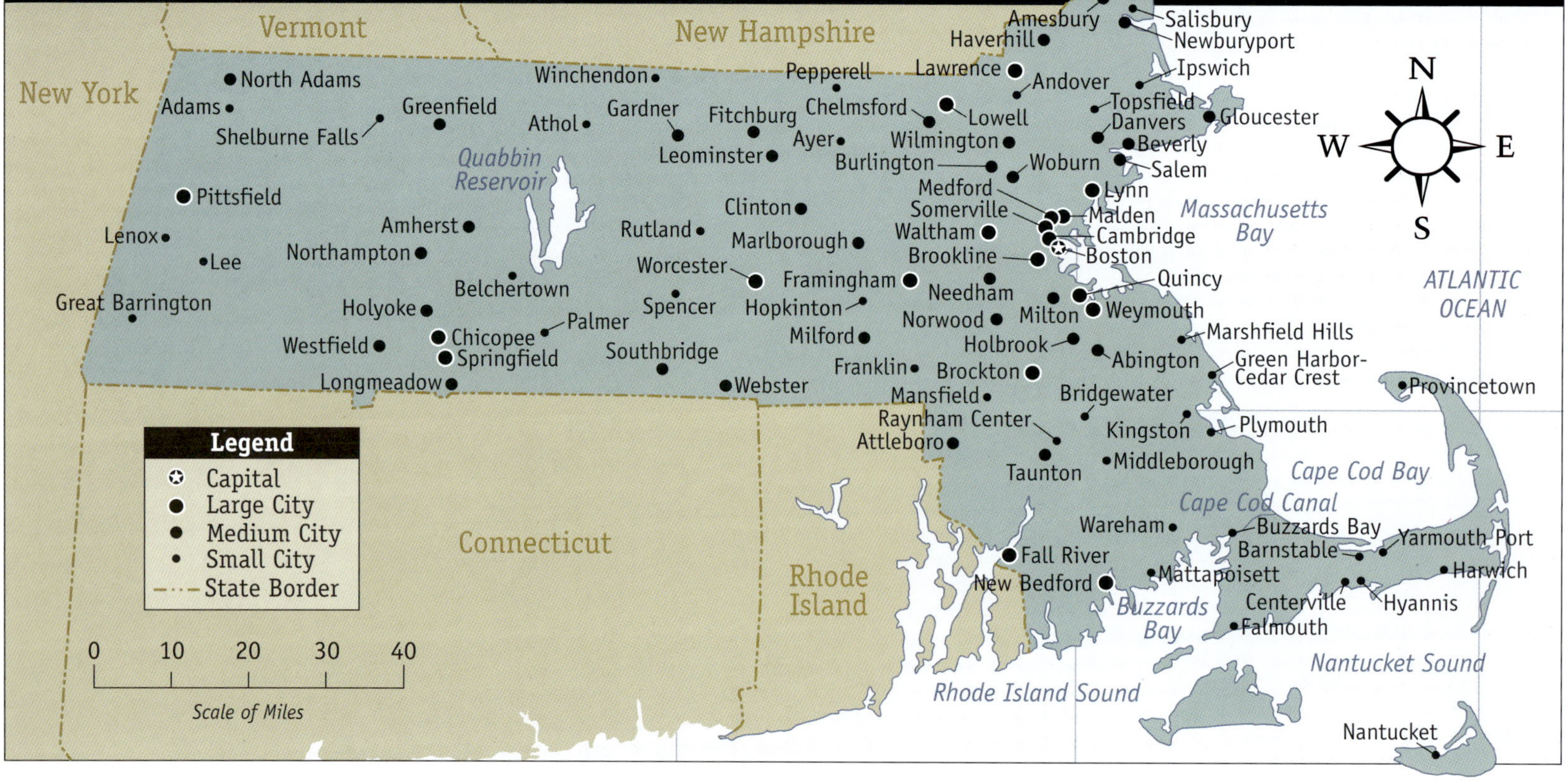

Glossary

The definitions given here are for the **Words to Understand** as they are used in this textbook. The words are highlighted in yellow where they are defined.

A

accuse: to blame
almanac: a book that tells about the weather, ocean tides, and movement of the sun, stars, and moon
amend: to change
ancestor: a relative who lived long ago
apprentice: a person who lives with a craftsman and learns his skills
artifact: something made or used by people of the past

B

banish: to send away
barter: the exchange of goods and services without using money
bayonet: a spear that fits on the end of a rifle
biography: the story of a person's life
blacksmith: a person who shapes iron into tools and other items
boycott: an act in which people stop buying something in order to make a point
brand: to mark by burning

C

cape: a point of land that juts out into a large body of water
cardinal directions: the directions on a compass: north, south, east, and west
cattail: a plant that grows in marshy areas
century: 100 years
ceramic: made of clay material and fired at a high temperature
challenge: a kind of test
character: a person's personality traits
citizen: a member of a city, state, or nation
civil rights: the rights that belong to every citizen
colony: a settlement in another country far away, ruled by the mother country
community: a group of people living and working together
congress: a group of representatives who meet to work out a problem
constellation: a pattern of stars
content: satisfied
cooperation: working together
council: a group of people who meet to talk about something
courage: bravery
cradleboard: a frame Native Americans used to carry babies on their backs
criticize: to find fault

D

decade: ten years
declaration: a letter, document, or statement that makes something known to everyone
defend: to protect
document: an official paper
drought: a long period of time when there is no rain

E

economics: the study of how people get the goods and services they need and want
encourage: to help or support
endangered species: a species of animals that is in danger of completely disappearing

engraving: a carved or cut figure or design
explorer: a person who goes to new places to learn about them

F

flattering: full of praise
flax: a plant with fibers that are used to make thread and other things
found: to start

G

geography: the study of Earth and the people, plants, and animals living on it
goods: things that people make to sell
gourd: a type of squash that is dried and used for bowls or rattles
govern: to make the rules
government: a person or group of people who rule or have control
governor: a political leader of a place
graze: to feed on grass or in a pasture
gristmill: a place where grain is ground into flour

H

harbor: a protected place near the shore where the water is deep enough for large ships
harvest: to gather crops
heroine: a woman who is admired and remembered for something she did
historic site: a place where history was made
history: the story of the past
hornbook: a wooden paddle with a sheet of paper attached to it that had words printed on it

I

inalienable: unable to be taken away
income: the money a person makes from working
independence: freedom from another's control
industrial: having to do with producing goods
influence: to have an effect on
interpreter: a person who explains something to people in another language
island: land surrounded by water on all sides

J

journal: a diary

L

landmark: something that stands out in a town
law: a rule
legacy: a gift to the future
liquid: fluid or flowing, like water
livestock: animals that are raised for their meat, eggs, or milk
local: close to home
local government: city or town government; government close to home
longhouse: a large Native American home made of saplings and bark
loom: a machine that weaves thread or yarn together to make cloth
Loyalist: a person who wanted the 13 colonies to remain loyal to England
lynch: to kill someone by mob violence, usually by hanging

M

manufacturing: the act of making something with machines
map legend: a key that shows what the symbols on a map stand for
massacre: the violent killing of many people
meetinghouse: a place where people could worship together or hold town meetings
merchant: a person who made a living by trading goods between the colonies and different countries
militia: a company of soldiers who protected a town
mill: a place where corn and wheat are ground into flour
minuteman: a colonist who could be ready in a few minutes to fight the British

mishoon: a Wampanoag word for a canoe made from a tree trunk
monadnock: a rocky hill or mountain standing alone
museum: a place where historical objects are put on display
musket: a gun
muster: a gathering of the militia to practice shooting or to be inspected

N

native: belonging to a place by birth
natural resource: something found in nature that people use

O

opinion: a belief or judgment
opportunity: the chance to do something
order: a state of peace

P

pamphlet: a printed paper about a topic
patent: an official paper that gives someone the right to something
patient: capable of waiting
Patriot: a person who wanted the 13 colonies to be independent from England
pension: money given to someone by the government
pewter: a type of tin used to make spoons, forks, cups, bowls, and pitchers
pillory: a wooden frame into which a person's head and hands were locked
pioneer: one of the first people to settle a place
pniese: a Wampanoag word for warrior
point of view: a way of seeing something
politics: the activities of the government
port: a place on the water where boats can dock
powwow: a Native American meeting or celebration
prejudice: making judgments about people because of their race or religion
printing press: a machine for printing from inked type, plates, or rolls
privacy: the state of being left alone
protest: to complain against an idea or an action
public: used by the people or community
public school: school that is paid for by all the people of a city or town, not just by the parents of the students who go there
publish: to prepare a document to be given to the public

R

recluse: a person who wants to be alone
representative: someone elected to speak, act, or vote for other people
reservoir: a lake made by people
respect: the state of being honored
revolution: a battle that people fight to replace one government with a different government
rights: privileges

S

sachem: a Native American leader
sapling: a young tree
scale of miles: a symbol on a map that represents actual distances
scarce: hardly
scholarship: money given to a student to pay for school
scurvy: a disease caused by not getting enough vitamin C
self-government: government in which people make the laws and agree to live by them
self-reliance: being able to do things for yourself
service: work that people do for other people to earn a living
sinew: a tendon that connects muscles and bones
slave: a person who is owned by another person and forced to work without pay
solid: firm or hard
specialization: the act of producing only one kind of product or being skilled at one job

state: a political region within a country
suburb: a place outside the city with houses, yards, and shopping malls
suffrage: the right to vote
surrender: to give up
survive: to stay alive
symbol: something that stands for something else

T

tan: to stretch an animal skin to make it lighter
tax: money people pay to the government
textile: cloth that is woven or knitted
time period: a chunk of time
trade: to give something in return for something else
trading post: a place where people meet to trade goods
tradition: a way of life handed down from one generation to the next
transportation: moving from place to place
treaty: a promise that is written down
trench: a ditch dug in the ground to protect soldiers during war
tribe: a community of Native Americans

U

unique: different

V

valley: low land between mountains and hills
volunteer: someone who gives his or her time to help others

W

wampum: beadwork made with tiny shells or stones
wetu: a Native American home made from wood, bark, and grasses
wharf: a place along the shore where ships dock to drop off and pick up cargo

Index

L

M

N

O

P

Q

R

S

T

U

V

W

Credits

Amherst College Archives & Special Collections by permission of the Trustees of Amherst College 172
Boston Public Library 175
Colonial Williamsburg Foundation 95
Emily Dickinson Museum, Amherst, Massachusetts 173
Fisher Museum, Harvard Forest, Petersham 103
Gary Rasmussen vi-vii, 8, 9, 42-43, 46, 47, 51, 52, 54 (top), 55, 61, 72, 88-89, 90, 109 (top), 137,161
Historic Deerfield 10, 94 (top)
James P. Rowan 53, 76, 80 (top left), 122 (Granary Burying Ground and Faneuil Hall), 123 (Bunker Hill Monument and Old State House), 147
Jean Crossman, Amherst History Museum 80 (bottom), 96 (top), 119 (top)
John Alley 48
John T. Kraft and Susan E. Finn 50
John Trumbull, *Patrick Tracy*, Image copyright Board of Trustees, National Gallery of Art, Washington 104
Jon Burton 66, 99, 140, 154-155, 159, 162-163
Kindra Clineff 2-3, 5, 11 (bottom), 14-15, 22 (top right), 26, 29 (left), 31, 35, 40-41, 56 (left), 59, 71, 75, 76 (left), 77, 78, 93, 115, 122 (Old South), 123 (Freedom Trail Sign), 144-145, 147 (bottom), 148, 157, 166-167, 171 (bottom)
Library of Congress 85 (middle), 102 (top), 111, 149, 151 (bottom), 168, 169, 170, 173, 174, 178, 179, 181
Lobster Pot Restaurant 25
Massachusetts Office of Tourism 11 (top), 27 (right), 76 (right), 146 (top), 150 (right), 153
Museum of Fine Arts, Boston 128
NASA 22 (world)
North Wind Picture Archives 62-63, 67, 68, 70, 82-83, 85 (top), 87, 106-107, 112-113, 114, 116, 118, 119 (bottom), 121, 127, 135, 136, 174 (bottom)
Photos.com 12, 17, 18 (left), 19 (top), 22, 25 (top), 48 (top), 50 (top), 64, 158
Pilgrim Hall Museum, Plymouth, Massachusetts 74
Pocumtuck Valley Memorial Association, Memorial Hall Museum, Deerfield, Massachusetts 7, 56 (bottom), 92, 94 (left)
Richard Cummins 34, 101, 182, 183
Saint-Gobain 28
Sarah Hatch 185
Shauna Kawasaki 6, 79, 143
Ski Butternut 33 (bottom right)
Suzanne Chappelle 19 (bottom)
Suzanne Chappelle, Irvine Nature Center 49
The Bostonian Society/Old State House 108
The Peabody Museum of Archaeology and Ethnology 44, 54 (bottom), 57
Tom Till 18 (top)
Wampanoag Tribe of Aquinnah, Education Department 58
William H. Johnson 24, 29 (top right), 30, 32-33